To Gerry —

Dreams Can and
Do Come True, if
you Can Just
Believe.

Willie Talley

IT ONLY TAKES A MINUTE TO CHANGE YOUR LIFE

WILLIE JOLLEY

Host of The Magnificent Motivational Minute

KENDALL/HUNT PUBLISHING COMPANY
4050 Westmark Drive   Dubuque, Iowa 52002

This book is dedicated to my wife Dee, who is not only my wife but also my best friend and most of all, my queen, whose love, support and hard work made this book a reality.
To my children, William and LaToya, for their love and support. To my mother Catherine B. Jolley, for her unending love, support and faith in me. To Rhonda Davis Smith and Darlene Bryant for their help and high standards as readers. Finally, this book is dedicated to the memory of my mother-in-law, Lillie Mae Taylor, who passed while I was writing this book, yet who continued to love, encourage, inspire and motivate me up until her death and continues to do so, even today. I Love You Always!

Willie Jolley

TABLE OF CONTENTS

FOREWORD
BY LES BROWN

I first met Willie Jolley during an appearance I made at Howard University in Washington, DC. As usual, at the end of my presentation, I took a few minutes for questions from the audience. A young man stepped up to the mike and said just a few words. I knew then there was something special about Willie Jolley and I asked him to stick around after the program so we could have a few words together. He promised he would.

This particular evening, I was swamped with people wanting interviews and autographs and my arrangement to meet Willie completely slipped my mind. An hour or so went by before I was able to return to my hotel where I was surprised and delighted to see Willie Jolley seated in the lobby, reading a book and armed with his ever-present smile. It took only a few minutes of talking with Willie before I knew for certain that he was a young man destined for greatness.

Since that time, I have seen Willie Jolley continue to grow, to strive for greatness and to dream the big dream . . . and to go after that dream. I've watched him grow from a well-received local speaker to one of the hottest young speaking talents in the country. When Willie told me about his book, I was excited. I know the level of enthusiasm that Willie invests in each project he undertakes, whether it is speaking, singing, hosting his radio show or just shaking your hand. This book is Willie Jolley at his best.

It Only Takes A Minute To Change Your Life is written the way Willie lives, with enthusiasm, excitement and energy. His book is full of inspirational and quickly-digested ideas, anecdotes and stories designed specifically for the person who's on-the-move and eager to get the most out of life. Read this book. Then re-read it. Experience the love and care that Willie has taken with each anecdote and example. Meditate on the stories and jump into the success exercises. Grab hold of the goal-setting techniques—then let them grab hold of you. Dream the big dream; think the big thought and dare to live life to the fullest.

Live your dream. Because you, like Willie Jolley, were destined for greatness! *It Only Takes A Minute To Change Your Life* . . . Enjoy the journey!

PREFACE

———— ▨ ————

"**G**reat things can come in small packages." We have all heard this statement many times. But I learned firsthand about the power of this statement a few years ago, when I was making my living as a singer and jazz musician. While in graduate school I supported myself by singing with various performers across the country. I would perform on weekends and go to school during the week. One of the best experiences I had was as a background singer with the great jazz artist, Jean Carne. When I first went out on the road with her I found that she was not only a great singer but was also very unselfish about sharing the stage with the background performers. During a portion of the show she would always introduce the band members and singers and give them a chance to show what they could do. This would be our time to solo and showcase our talents. The problem was that because of the number of people in the band, we were asked to keep our solos to eight measures.

Surprisingly, most of them couldn't do it. They could not keep their solos to eight measures. They could not conceive that a great performance could be given in just eight measures. Most of them would just start warming up at the eight-measure mark and would take so long that the band leader would just have to cut them off because they took too much time, which was very embarrassing. I was the new kid on the block and definitely did not want to be embarrassed. I studied the other people and I made up my mind that I was going to create an entertaining and exciting eight-measure performance. I figured I needed to make it short and sweet to get the maximum out of a minimum amount of time. So when it was my turn I delivered a solo that had a beginning, a middle and an ending. It involved the audience in a call and response, then a sing-song where I sang a quick rap and rhyme, then closed with a big finale, all in eight measures! It was a big hit and immediately became a popular part of the show. Well, from that experience I learned it doesn't take a long time to make a positive impression or to get your point across. It's not important how much time you have, the key is what you do with the time you've got.

That experience taught me that with limited time, you must make the best of what you've got to work with. It taught me the importance and power of brevity. It taught me that great performances can be short and succinct. In fact, one of the greatest performances of all time was one of the shortest. It was a speech given by Abraham Lincoln at the Gettysburg battlefield, the Gettysburg Address. A short speech, less than five minutes, yet it has been called one of the greatest speeches of all times. In fact, the principal speaker for that Gettysburg program, Edward Everett, said he wished he had been as effective in two hours as Lincoln had been in five minutes!

It does not take a long time to make a point, give a message or, in fact, to change a life—It Only Takes A Minute. As I progressed through life I remembered that lesson. Later, I started singing jingles and performing for commercials. I had sixty seconds to tell my story and sell the product. Again, I used the same concept and learned to deliver my message in a short period of time. The ability to tell the story quickly kept me quite busy as a jingle singer.

I didn't forget the concept when I started speaking and decided to develop some programs that would appeal to an audience in a short period of time. I envisioned programs that were informational, motivational, inspirational and entertaining yet short and compact. I wanted to give a lot in a little bit of time. Time is very precious, and people are always rushing. They need motivation and often they need it in a hurry. The result was "The Magnificent Motivational Minute" radio series, one-minute motivational messages that are entertaining, informational, inspirational and motivational.

This book is written to share that concept with readers. It contains stories and thoughts that are designed to be short and quick but to give a lasting impression; ideas that are designed to give the maximum in a minimum time. In an age of minute rice, instant coffee, fast food, quick cash and phone loans, we now are happy to present minute motivation. The Magnificent Motivational Minute Book: "It Only Takes A Minute To Change Your Life."

As my friend James Carter, the success strategist says, "This book is designed to help you take the tip from the top, the drip from the drop and to be the cream of the crop!"

INTRODUCTION
BY *W MITCHELL*

T he *power of positive thinking* is hardly a new idea. The concept of *motivation* hasn't just burst on the scene. But Willie Jolley packages both of these ideas in a brand new way, injecting these power-packed motivational messages with his unflagging energy and enthusiasm. For years, Willie has offered his radio audience a bright spot in their day; a little caffeine for the spirit. His *Magnificent Motivational Minutes* have encouraged his listeners and inspired them to pursue their dreams and take control of their lives.

Many of us in the hectic, fast-paced field of public speaking have been using these minute motivators as a resource for years. In the very little time we have between planes and between speeches, we're able to get a lot of information, inspiration and comfort from the messages that Willie Jolley has for us.

For as many years as Willie has been brightening the airwaves, his listeners have been begging him to share his insight with them in written form. This book, a compilation of Willie's *Magnificent Motivational Minutes,* his personal reflections and some terrific stories and ideas, is Willie's answer to those requests. Whether you dip into it a minute at a time or read it cover to cover in one sitting . . . you'll find yourself more inspired, more determined and more thoughtful with every page. Even if you have only a minute, who knows, in that minute you might just change your life. The most important thing in any project . . . is TO BEGIN. The old Chinese proverb says that the longest journey always begins with a single step. By making sure that you read the first page of this book, you will get to page two. Read the first page, take the first step and begin the journey and by the time you get to a few pages in this book you will be running and on your way . . . To reach your dreams. Do It Now! ALOHA!

A Personal Note From Willie Jolley

———————— ▨ ————————

For so many years I thought, as do most people, that a minute was an insignificant amount of time. I figured that the only significant use for a minute was just to make hours, which were more important. I would hear people say, "I'll be there in a minute" or "Wait a minute" when they really didn't mean a minute. They were actually talking about 10, 15, 20 minutes or longer. A minute was just a figure of speech, something that we all took for granted.

As I grew older I realized that great things can come in small packages. I realized that a minute was not only vital, but it was the starting point of all success. We must be mindful of the fact that, just as pennies create dollars, minutes create hours. The difference is that if you throw away your pennies you have the capability to make more, as many as you want. But your time is not the same: you have a limit on the time you have on this earth, a limit on the number of minutes that you have to live. You must therefore be mindful of time and respectful of the minutes that make the hours, that make the days, that make the months, that ultimately make the years, because they are limited. Once lost, a minute cannot be recaptured. What you do with your minutes will ultimately determine what you do with your life.

In fact, time is probably the only commodity on this earth that is equally distributed, the only thing that no person has as an advantage over another. We all have 24 hours to each day, 1440 minutes. No one is given an hour more or an hour less. Everyone has 24 hours and there is absolutely nothing anyone can do to add more time to the day. It does not matter how much money you have or how much influence you command. The richest of the rich and the poorest of the poor have the same amount of time. The key to success is how we use that time.

If we think of time in relation to water we can see that most of us do not really think much of a single drop of water. But when that single drop of water is connected with more single drops of water it can become a raging river and when harnessed can be one of the most powerful forces on this earth. The same is true for minutes: singularly they are not highly considered, but in each minute is the potential for greatness. And when these minutes are harnessed and wisely used, they too can generate great power. It only takes a minute to change your life!

One of the major things that pushed me to write this book was the response I received from the listeners of my daily radio program. I was amazed at the numbers of people who contacted me by phone or mail or just stopped me on the street. These people were excited about the concept of short, quick motivational ideas, "Minute Motivation." They told their friends and the station got more and more calls and letters about the show. I received numerous calls from listeners who wanted a copy of one script or another. The idea of putting together a book of the scripts crossed my mind, but it was just not a priority.

One day I received a letter from a young lady whose life had been changed by the motivational minute, and her letter had a major affect on me. This young lady had recently graduated from college and was having no success in finding a job. She was looking and looking, getting no positive responses and becoming more and more despondent. She got to the point where she was in a state of total depression, so far down that she just didn't see a reason for getting out of bed in the morning. She would stay in bed and sleep all day, for she felt there was no use trying anymore. She felt it was a hopeless situation.

One morning while lying in bed she heard the motivational minute on the radio. She said she experienced something that morning that created a spark and made her see life a little differently. That motivational minute became my trademark story and has become one of my most inspirational and popular shows, called "The Lion and The Gazelle". It changed her life!

THE LION AND THE GAZELLE

Today's step for success is that we must see every day as an opportunity which demands that we give our all, do our best. We must see success not only as a destination but as a journey that is constantly filled with adventure and challenges. And if we are willing to meet those challenges, then we can live life to the fullest. I want to share with you a story I recently heard. Every morning in Africa a gazelle wakes up and knows that it must run faster than the fastest lion or it will be killed and eaten. Also every morning in Africa a lion wakes up and knows that it must outrun the slowest gazelle or it will starve to death. It doesn't matter whether you are a lion or a gazelle, when the sun comes up, you'd better be running! Remember that all things are possible if you can just believe! Have a great day.

She heard the show that morning and realized she had to make a decision. It made her believe she could not only get a job, but she could get the job she wanted, if she wanted it badly enough and was willing to make it happen. She got up and got started working toward her goal, and began listening to the show every day. And every day she got stronger and stronger and more committed to making her dreams come true. Initially she had no success in her search, but she did not give up because she now had a new determination, a new mind set. Within a few weeks, not only did she find a job, but she found one in her field which paid her more than she had originally been seeking!

She wrote me a wonderful letter and asked if I would send her the written copies of the scripts so she could read them and share them with her friends and family. I realized at that moment it was imperative that I make the time to compile these scripts and share them with others, because people are desperately in need of motivation and encouragement. There is a great hunger for positive information. Yet, in the hectic pace of our day-to-day lives, people need quick, short ways of getting motivation. They need instant motivation, motivation in a minute. So now I am happy to present motivation in a minute, because it really only takes a minute, just a minute . . . to change your life!

My goal is that this book will help you make the decision to take the initial action to change your life. My objective is that after you read this book you will have a new mind set, a new determination; you will be a new person. How? Well, it has been stated that a mind once stretched by new ideas can never return to its original position. I hope this book will stretch your mind to attain new ideas and get you to reach deeper within yourself to pursue your dreams. No matter how successful you are or how much you have achieved thus far, I hope this will motivate you to continue to push to accomplish even more. I hope to show you that every minute is precious and every minute is a gift, packed with power, and every minute has the potential to change your life . . . if you use it wisely!

THE IMPORTANCE OF A SINGLE MINUTE!

―――――――――― 🔲 ――――――――――

Kipling wrote, "Fill the unforgiving minute with 60 seconds worth of distance run." Sixty seconds worth of distance run means to use your time wisely for the minute is very unforgiving. It does not care who you are or what your position is; it is unforgiving for you, for me, for the President, Members of Congress, doctors, lawyers and everyone else. Time waits for no one, so we must be mindful of our minutes and realize they are probably the most precious commodity we possess. Once spent, they cannot be replaced.

Each person on this earth is given a measure of time to live and this time is limited. Each person also is given a daily measure of time, the hours of each day, which is absolutely the same for everybody. Rich people have no more time per day than poor people; short people have no more time than tall people; kings and queens have no more time than any of the common people in their kingdoms. Each person is given 24 hours each day, 1440 minutes that are credited to that person's account. When those minutes have been spent, you cannot buy any more minutes that day. When your day is over, when those 1440 minutes have been used you cannot purchase any more time, no matter how much money you have or how much power you possess.

TIME IS MOVING, ARE YOU?

Friends, time waits for no one. It moves on and keeps moving on. It does not stop for anything or anybody. It doesn't matter how much money you have, how much power you have or how much prestige you have, time keeps moving on. Therefore you have got to respect time and use it wisely, because time doesn't care who you are. Time is the great equalizer. From its standpoint everybody is equal. It gives the same dividend to the rich and to the poor, to the powerful and to the weak, to the big and to the small. Everybody has the same amount of time, 24 hours per day, not one minute more. The key to success is not the time you have, because you've only got 24 hours, 1440 minutes to each day; the key is what you do with the time you have. How do you use your time? Do you use it wisely or do you squander your precious minutes? Do you fill your life with time a-wasting, or do you fill your time with life a-making? Your success or your failure depends on how you use your time. Time is moving on . . . are you?

Each minute is precious because it cannot be replaced. Once this day has been spent, we cannot change the time that has gone by. Each day is its own separate unit of time and cannot be relived. Once gone, it is over and done with, so we must use it wisely, because we have no guarantee how much time we have on this earth.

MAKE YOUR MINUTES WORK FOR YOU

We all have 24 hours per day, not a minute more or a minute less. The key to success is what you're doing with the minutes you are given. My friend Mike Murdock says we all have 24 boxcars that we are given each day. Do you fill them with dirt or with diamonds? Donald Trump has 24 hours every day; so does my friend Bobby, the window washer. The difference is how they use the time they have. Bobby is a man who washes people's windows at my local gas station in exchange for their spare change. He is very articulate and very personable, but he has resigned himself to being a window washer because he doesn't believe he can do any better. He has had some tough circumstances and has simply given up and thrown in the towel. Every time we talk he always says, "I'm gonna do it, I'm gonna do it," but he never does. The next day he is back there washing windows for pennies, when he has the potential to make dollars. He fills his minutes with dirt when he could have diamonds. Donald Trump, on the other hand, also has 24 hours, but he uses his time differently. He fills his minutes with dollars rather than pennies. Life is difficult for us all, and offers unique challenges to each person. Some start off further behind than others, but each of us can choose how we spend our time. Do we fill our hours with dirt or with diamonds? Do we fill our minutes with dimes or with dollars? No matter where we are in life, we do have a choice. Use your time wisely. Fill your time with diamonds and not dirt!

How long does it take to change your life? Most people believe that it takes a long time, but that is a myth! In reality it only takes a minute. That's right, a minute! The minute you actually decide to change and decide to move in a different direction is the minute that you actually change your life. What takes a long time is getting ready to make a decision! You bounce around the ideas whether you should or you shouldn't, trying to debate the issue of change. Many debate and think so long on an idea that they are caught up in the "paralysis of analysis." They debate it so long that nothing actually gets done. But the minute you decide and take action is the minute you actually change your life. Dr. Howard Thurman, the great theologian, stated, "The moment, the minute that this generation conquers fear, then that is the minute that the battle is won . . . the skirmishes will come, but the battle is won!" The moment, the minute we make the decision is the minute we change our lives!

THE IMPORTANCE OF A SINGLE MINUTE

Today we want to talk about the importance of a single minute, this minute you are investing in reading this page. It may not seem like a big deal, but let me tell you it is a major deal, because a minute is the starting point of building your dreams. From a great minute comes a great hour, and from a great hour comes a great day, and from a great day comes a great week, then a great month, then a great year, and from there you can be the architect of a great lifetime! And it starts with a single minute. That is why we must cherish every minute and use our minutes wisely. Dr. Benjamin Mays said it best:

> I have only just a minute, only 60 seconds in it.
> Forced upon me, can't refuse it. Didn't seek it,
>   didn't choose it,
> But it's up to me to use it,
> I must suffer if I lose it, give account if I abuse it.
> Just a tiny little minute, but an eternity is in it.
> So ladies and gentlemen, use your minutes
>   wisely.

What is motivation? Motivation is taken from the latin word *motere,* which means to take action. I personally like to think of motivation as having three specific parts, which I have stated for this book in a very simple way.

CONCEIVE IT, BELIEVE IT AND ACHIEVE IT!

Welcome to the Magnificent Motivational Minute, a minute that will inform, inspire, educate and motivate. A minute that can change your life. To fully understand the motivational minute, let's first define motivation. Webster defines motivation as something that drives or causes a person to act. I see motivation as having three parts. First is to get you to dream, to conceive of a concept. Second is to get you to believe in your heart; the Bible says that all things are possible if you can just believe. The third part is to get you to do something, to go after your dreams, to pursue your dreams and then to achieve your dreams. In short, to motivate you is to help you understand that if you can conceive it and believe it, then you can achieve it. If you can dream it, you can do it. You can be great. Remember that all things are possible if you can just believe.
Have a fantastic day!

DREAM IT,
THEN DO IT!

H ave you ever wondered why some people can make a million
dollars and lose it, make a second million and lose it, then
make a third million, while others can hardly make ends
meet? Why is it that some people, no matter what they touch, it seems
to turn to gold, while others can never quite hit the mark? The answer
is that those people know the recipe for success. Just as there is a
recipe for a cake or pie, there is also a recipe for success. You all know
someone who can make great cakes and pies, like my wife's Aunt
Bubba. Aunt Bubba makes the best cakes, pies and rolls I have ever
tasted, and she makes them almost every day. Sometimes she has to
double the quantity because people eat them up so quickly. But no
matter how fast the pies and the rolls are eaten, she can make more
because she has the recipe.

Now, let's say someone comes to my aunt's house and loves the
way the cakes and pies taste. So this person decides that he is going to
go home and make some for himself, but he does not have the recipe.
So he goes home and tries and fails, then he tries again and fails, and
tries and fails and tries and fails and eventually, like most people, he
gives up. Well, that's what happens in life. Most people want to be successful, but they don't have the recipe. Most people go through life in a

constant state of trial and error; they try and fail, then try and fail and try and fail and eventually they give up. Statistics show that if you take 100 people and start them at the same place at the age of 19, by the time they are 65 only one will be wealthy, 4 will be financially secure, 19 will still be working to simply survive, and 54 will be flat broke and dependent on the government or their families for their survival. It doesn't have to be that way!

What do all successful people have in common? Ninety-nine percent of the time I get the same answer . . . money! It is the number one answer whether I go to schools, colleges, trade associations or corporations. It is the number one answer, but it is not the right answer! Money does not determine your success, but if you are successful you can have as much money as you need. Case in point: Mother Teresa is a major success, but she has no money. Martin Luther King, Jr., was a major success, but he was not a rich man. I had a teacher in junior high school who was always encouraging and inspiring me, no matter how much I misbehaved. Every day she would say to our class, "You're gonna be great, you're gonna be great!" That school teacher is not a rich woman, but she is a major success, many of her students have gone on to do exceptional things.

Money in itself does not determine success, but if you're successful you can have as much money as you need. If Mother Teresa were to go on television at noon on any day of the week and make a worldwide appeal for $50 million, she would have it before the end of that day. Money does not determine success, but if you are successful you can have as much money as you need.

What is the common denominator, the main ingredient for all success? It is the ability TO DREAM! To see things that are not yet a reality as being a possibility. To be able to dream is be able to develop a vision for your future. The Bible says in Proverbs 29:15, "Where there is no vision the people perish." Dreams are essential for success; no matter what else you have or don't have, one thing you must have is a dream. As the lyrics from one of the songs in the broadway production, South Pacific say, "You gotta have a dream, you gotta have a dream. If you don't have a dream, how you gonna have a dream come true?" Friends, you've got to have a dream!

STANDING ON THE VERGE; YOU GOTTA DREAM!

As I travel around the country speaking, there is one point I cannot stress enough. It is the importance of dreaming, the need to dream. In interviews with great people around the world, one common element consistently comes up: they all have the ability to dream. From Martin Luther King, Jr., to Walt Disney, to Thomas Edison, to Albert Einstein, the list goes on and on and on. Dreams are the seeds for success. We're going to learn how to dream those dreams that change our lives. We'll learn how to dream, how to follow our dreams, and how to make them come true. If you can dare to dream, then you can dare to win. I'm excited because we are standing on the verge of a great adventure, and it's called living life to the fullest. Get ready, set, go! Let's start to dream! And as always have a great day.

THE IMPORTANCE OF IMAGINATION

The importance of imagination was impressed upon me as a youth, when I had the opportunity to meet Muhammad Ali. I was visiting my grandmother in Philadelphia and my mother was able to get tickets to see Muhammad Ali at the taping of a local television show. I was so excited I didn't know what to do, I couldn't wait until it was time to go the television studio. We arrived and we even got front row seats! The champ arrived and shook everybody's hand on the front row, and I was so excited because I could now go home and tell all of my friends that I actually shook hands with Muhammad Ali!

I look back now and realize that shaking his hand was fine, but it would wear off. But during the interview he said something that changed my life and would not wear off. He planted a seed that grew as I grew and helped to shape my thinking. During the interview he was asked how he had revolutionized the boxing industry so that people flocked to see his fights. He replied that he had imagination and that was the key to his success. He said, "You see, I learned a long time ago that being good was simply not good enough; you've got to have imagination and you've got to dream." He developed a personality, a persona, that people either loved or they hated. Those who loved him came to see him win; those who hated him came to see him lose. Either way, every seat was taken! I learned on that day that you have to have imagination, you've got to be creative, you've got to have a dream!

THE DREAMSEED

Just as everything in life that grows is the result of a seed, the same is true for your dreams. Dreams are the starting point for success, the seeds for success. If you take a corn seed, plant it and water it daily, it will grow into a corn stalk. If you take an acorn, plant it and water it daily, it will grow into an oak tree. The same is true for your dreams. If you can conceive the dream in your mind, plant it in your heart and water it daily, then it too will grow. How do you water it? You water it by saying daily, "I believe I can; I believe I can; in fact I know can." Plant your dream deep, water it daily, and don't let the weeds of doubt choke it, and your dream can and will become a reality.

· · · · · · · · · ·■━━━━━━━━━■· · · · · · · · · ·

THE DREAMER,
MICHAEL JORDAN

One of my favorite examples of a dreamer is Michael Jordan. I once heard a story about Michael Jordan that began by asking, "What made him such a great basketball player?" The answer was this: When he was in the ninth grade he got cut from the basketball team for not being good enough. He went home and started to dream of doing impossible things with a basketball, because he wanted to prove to the coach that he had made a mistake. Once Michael could dream and see it in his mind, then he realized he could do it. And once he realized he could do it, he went out on the court and did it! He dreamed it and he did it and he became a great basketball player. When he retired he said he had no more desire to play basketball because he had achieved his dream, to be the best, and he wanted to move on to his other dreams. He understands that in life, to be great is to always be willing to pursue your dreams. The key to success is to dream and then to go after those dreams. Then you too can reach the sky!

• • • • • • • •● ■■■■■■■■■■■ ●• • • • • • • •

You've Got To Have A Dream!

Every day is a brand new day, a day unlike any other day, a brand new opportunity to make your dreams come true. But in order for your dreams to come true, it is necessary for you to have a dream. You've got to have a dream, a goal. Not just a resolution that you make on the first of January and forget by the fifteenth, but a goal, a target, a destination that you have made a commitment to. It is critical that you have a dream. Dr. Benjamin Mays said it so well: "It must be borne in mind that the tragedy of life doesn't lie in not reaching your goal. The tragedy lies in not having a goal to reach for. It isn't a calamity to die with dreams unfulfilled, but it is a calamity not to dream. It is not a disaster to be unable to capture your ideal, but it is a disaster to have no ideal to capture. It is not a disgrace not to reach the stars, but it is a disgrace to have no stars to reach for. Not failure, but low aim, is sin!" Ladies and gentlemen, most people have low aim or no aim and make little resolutions that they don't stick to. If you aim at nothing, that is probably what you will hit! Aim high, dream big dreams, set big goals and remember, all things are possible if you can just believe.

HANK AARON, DREAMING IN SLOW MOTION!

In an interview with Hank Aaron, author Robert Griessman stated that Aaron was not just an exceptional athlete, but also used other tools to help him to become the top home run hitter of all time. He used his ability to dream in combination with an exceptional ability to focus and concentrate. Mr. Griessman says that Hank Aaron would study pitchers throughout the league and concentrate on their strengths and weaknesses. He would then focus on what it would take for him to hit home runs off them. Last, but not least, he would dream about the game and envision himself seeing the ball and focusing on it until he could control the speed of the ball in his thoughts, and then he could make it slow down right as it approached the plate! He would then hit the ball with all of his power and the result would be . . . a home run. He would combine the ability to dream with extreme focus; he would see home runs as a possibility, then he would make them into realities!

I was recently speaking to a group of young people and one young lady told me she was confused because she had dreams every night, and she hadn't seen any major difference in her life; she wasn't a success yet. I explained to her that there are different types of dreams. One is the type you have at night where you just see pictures and stories in your mind. There are the good ones where everything is wonderful, and then there are the bad ones, which we commonly call nightmares. (Some of the young people laughed and said they liked nightmares because they got to see a free scary movie without having to leave home, leave their beds or even get up and turn on the television.)

Another type of dream is the daydream, where you drift off into far-away thoughts while you are still awake. Most times this happens in school or while you are at work, when you are supposed to be paying attention to someone or something else. The problem with daydreaming is that it is hard to learn or accomplish much when your body is in one place and your mind is in another. The last kind of dream is the one that makes the difference between success and failure: the dream to imagine.

THE DREAM TO IMAGINE!

The type of dream that we want to concentrate on today is the kind of dream that was exhibited by Dr. Martin Luther King, Jr.: the dream to imagine. To see things as a possibility that are not yet a reality. We are capable of unbelievable things if we allow our minds to soar, if we can cut away the binds that limit us. If you stop and look around you right now, everything you see started in someone's imagination. The radio you listen to, the clothes you wear, the telephone you speak on, your home, your car, your office. These things didn't exist thousands of years ago, but thanks to someone's imagination, they exist today. You too can use your imagination to do great things.

I HAVE A DREAM

Martin Luther King, Jr., gave a famous speech called "I Have A Dream." We have all heard those powerful words and his soul-stirring, passionate delivery that is timeless in its ability to inspire. In fact, no matter how often I hear that speech, I always get goosebumps because of the power that emanates from it. But as I was listening I started to think and realized the pure importance of these four words: I-have-a-dream, I-have-a-dream. It doesn't say I *had* a dream, but rather I *have* a dream. Why? Because to be great your dream must be ongoing. To say "I had a dream" implies that the dream has come and gone. But to have a dream means that it is ongoing, it is continuous. Do you have a dream? Is there a dream burning in your mind and spirit that consumes you and drives you to pursue it, and to eventually achieve it? I also noticed that Dr. King did not say, "I have a wish." Why? Because wishes have no substance and are usually unattainable. Like those who say "I wish I could live my life over again," or "I wish I were a child again." Most of us have thrown pennies into a wishing well or wished upon a star and never really expected those wishes to come true. They were just our fantasies. But a dream has substance. We dream of losing weight or buying a home or one day becoming the President of the United States. Dreams can and do come true! Don't be confused between a wish and a dream. Dream big dreams, think big thoughts and know all things are possible if you can just believe!

One of the other questions I get frequently from young people is, "Why dream?" Why dream? Good question. I recently read about a study in which college students were hooked up to machines that monitored their sleep patterns and brain waves to determine when they were dreaming. Dreams occur during rapid eye movement (R.E.M.) sleep. Every time the students started R.E.M. sleep patterns and the monitors registered they were starting to dream, they were awakened. They had a reasonable amount of sleep but were not allowed to dream. After the first night, the students woke up feeling irritable, after the second night they woke up edgy, after the third night they woke up irrational, and after the fourth night they woke up psychotic and the experiment was stopped. The study proved that it is critical to dream while you are asleep. But it is also critical to dream while you are awake!

WHERE DO DREAMS COME FROM?

Dreams, where do they come from? Robert Schuller, noted minister and author, says that dreams do not come out of the blue but rather come out of the mind of God. God matches the dream with the dreamer, someone who will receive it, respect it, embrace it, claim it, live for it and be willing to die for it. God gives to humans one of his greatest gifts, a dream. Yet it is up to us to receive it and let it grow, or to reject it and kill it. Proverbs 29:18 says, "Where there is no vision the people perish." We must dare to dream and dare to win.

I was speaking at Hampton University when one freshman asked a profound question: "How do you dream, when you cannot see a way out and you just can't see much hope?" And I have found that many people have given up on their dreams; they don't even remember how to dream and therefore don't think that they have a dream.

The Enemy On The Inside

You may ask why I spend so much time talking about dreams. Dreams are essential to success. Yet many people reject their dreams and are in reality their own worst enemies. How many of us have been given a thought, a dream or a vision and we've talked ourselves out of it by saying, "I can't do that, I just can't do that"? You can do anything you want to do! An old African proverb says, if you can overcome the enemy on the inside, the enemy on the outside won't be able to do you any harm. God would not give you a dream that you could not achieve. If you can dream it, then you can do it. If you are willing to accept it, conceive and believe it . . . then you can achieve it!

IF YOU CAN DREAM IT . . .

Walt Disney said, "If you can dream it, you can do it." He didn't just say it because it was a nice sounding phrase. He said it because he knew from personal experience that it was true. Walt Disney started as a simple cartoonist and went on to become one of the most successful entrepreneurs of all time. He went from dropping out of school to joining the army, to coming home and starting a business to drawing cartoons. The business failed and Walt went broke and had to sell everything to get enough money to get a one-way ticket to California. He went with $40, an imitation leather suitcase, one mismatched suit and some drawing materials, but he also had a dream. He arrived in California and started a new company which had some successes but also had some failures. He had setbacks and had two nervous breakdowns, but he still had a dream. Eventually he had to sell his car and mortgaged his home to start Disneyland, but he still had a dream. He borrowed to the hilt and was turned downed by lots and lots of people, but he still had a dream, and he believed in his dream. Disneyland became the biggest attraction in America and he became a multi-millionaire. If you can dream it, you can do it!

GOTTA DREAM

I have found that a dream mixed with confidence, determination, persistence and massive belief will grow into a reality. The bigger the dream, the bigger the rewards. Martin Luther King, Jr., had a dream. He was confident, determined and persistent. He became great. Mary McLeod Bethune had a dream. She wanted to start a college for black students who normally would not be able to attend a school of higher education. She started the school in Daytona Beach, Florida, with only six dollars to her name. But she was in possession of something more powerful—a dream. Today Bethune Cookman College is one of the greatest schools of higher education in this country and Mary McLeod Bethune is remembered as one of the greatest women this country has ever seen. She believed in her dream and had confidence, determination and persistence.

Spud Webb is five feet, six inches tall. He wanted to play basketball, but everyone said he was too short, that it could never happen. But Spud Webb had a dream, a big dream. A few years ago Spud Webb won the dunk contest for the National Basketball Association. Jose Feliciano was born blind in Puerto Rico, at a time when blind people were told they were not able to do anything but get a silver cup and beg for money. But Jose refused to accept that idea. He had a dream, a big dream. Jose found an old piece of guitar and taught himself how to play. He practiced day and night and night and day, sometimes until his fingers bled. Today Jose Feliciano is one of the greatest musicians the world has ever known. He wrote a song we sing every Christmas called *Feliz Navidad.* He is a multi-millionaire. You've got to have a dream. What is your dream? Whatever it is, you can achieve it . . . if you believe it, and have confidence, determination and persistence!

• • • • • • • • ••• ▬▬▬▬▬ •• • • • • • • •

THE MIND IS A MARVEL, USE IT!

Psychologists and doctors for years have said that we only use a small percentage of our mental capacity. Some say we only use about 15 percent of what the mind is capable of. The mind is like a movie camera and can replay things that have happened in the past, which is our memory. But it can also pre-play things that are going to happen in the future, which are our dreams! We all know how to replay our past, but very few know how to "pre-play" the future and how to make those dreams come true. If we can learn to dream and then dare to go after those dreams, we can do great things. Use all of your mind, and remember all things are possible if you can just believe!

• • • • • • • •• ▬▬▬▬▬ ••• • • • • • •

Resolutions, Or Just A Waste Of Time?

Many people make lots of New Year's resolutions. The problem is that they usually only last a couple of weeks. Statistics show that the sale of diet products and health club attendance are highest in the first two weeks of the year. People are motivated the first days of January and are really into their resolutions, but the enthusiasm starts to dwindle by the fifteenth of the month and usually fizzles out by the end of the month. Why? Because of a lack of continuous motivation. They get motivated at the first of the year but don't keep it up. Some people say the problem with motivation is that it wears off. Well, so does bathing! But you've made it a part of your daily routine to bathe every day. To make your resolutions into realities it is essential that you make motivation a part of your daily routine. Read or listen to something motivational. Fill your mind with the pure, the positive, the powerful. Find something (a book, a tape or song), that encourages and inspires you to dream and then motivates you to go after your dreams. And I recommend that you make this, the motivational minute, a part of your daily routine. It will help you to grow, help you to focus and help you to stay motivated. Ladies and gentlemen, remember that it only takes a minute to change your life! You must invest in yourself, if you want your dreams to come true. Have a great day!

Once you get a dream, is that all there is to it? No! It is not enough just to have a dream, you must follow the dream and make it into a reality. The dream is just the beginning. To make it into a reality you have to accept it, believe it, and then go after it.

FOLLOW YOUR DREAMS

We've been talking about the importance of dreams, that dreams are the seeds for success and are the starting place for achieving your goals. But you must remember once you get a dream, you've got to follow it. This verse by Gary Chergges says it so aptly:

> Follow your dream, wherever it leads.
> Don't be distracted by less worthy needs.
> Shelter it, nourish it, help it to grow.
> Let your heart hold it, down deep where dreams go.
> Follow your dream, pursue it with haste,
> Life is too precious, too fleeting to waste.
> Be fruitful, be loyal, and all the day through,
> The dream that you follow will keep coming true.

Once you conceive your dream and you believe it and nourish it, it will start to grow. But then you've got to be concerned about the weeds that will crop up all around your dream and start to kill it, strangle it, choke it! I like to call those weeds "the dreambusters". The dreambusters are very similar to ghostbusters. A ghostbuster's job is to kill, destroy, eliminate, get rid of the ghost. The dreambuster's job is to kill, destroy, eliminate, get rid of your dreams.

The difference is that ghostbusters are highly identifiable; they stand out in a crowd. They have proton packs, zappers, funny cars and funny clothes and that funny music which follows them everywhere they go. You can tell a ghostbuster a mile away. Dreambusters, though, are different. They do not stand out in a crowd and they have no identifiable characteristics. In fact, they look a whole lot like your best friend, classmate, co-worker, cousin or someone in your own household.

Once you find a dreambuster, you have two options: one, is to try to change them into "dream-makers"; inspire, encourage and enlighten them to the possibilities that exist. If this does not work, then you've only got one other option: LEAVE THEM ALONE! Get as far away from them as north is to south and east is to west. Get away and stay away because if you don't, they will bust your dreams and take you down with them!

There are many types of dreambusters, but there are four major dreambusters that are common and active in killing dreams today. The first is dulling influences (like drugs and alcohol), anything that dulls the senses and consistently keeps you from being sharp. The second is hanging out with negative people, particularly those who like to use the word CAN'T. The third is fear, letting fear shackle and strangle your initiative to try. The last major dreambuster is settling for mediocrity, when excellence is just a few steps away. This dreambuster is commonly seen in our young people who believe the lie that being smart is being a nerd! It is manifested in our adults who settle for mediocrity in their jobs and rationalize it by saying "It's close enough for government work," or "hospital work" or another kind of close enough. Why settle for close enough when excellence can be achieved with just a little bit more effort? Strive for excellence. Invest in it, and it will pay great dividends!

EXCELLENCE MAKES THE DIFFERENCE

In America we live in a pyramid society, where there are lots of people at the bottom of the pyramid and a few at the top. The people at the bottom are barely making ends meet from day to day, simply living from hand to mouth. The people at the top are those who are prospering and thriving. In every community and every geographic area there are lots of people at the bottom and a few people at the top. Many of the people at the top started at the bottom, among the masses, but rose to the top. Why? Because they refused to settle for mediocrity. They pursued excellence and began to rise. It's the "crème de la crème" principle: the cream will rise to the top. I recently saw Oprah Winfrey on an interview show and she was asked how she had risen from a broken home to her status as the most powerful woman in television. Her answer was that she pursued excellence in everything she did. She did not look like a television or movie star but she pursued excellence, and excellence is like truth, you cannot keep it down. You can push excellence down and try to cover it up and try to ignore it, but no matter what you do to it, it will always rise to the top! We must always pursue excellence in all that we do. Strive for excellence and your dreams will start to rise to the top!

Hammer . . . Why Not?

I recently had the opportunity to meet the rap artist Hammer. During our conversation I inquired if it was true what I had read about him in Readers Digest. He said it was true, very true. Ten years ago Mr. Hammer was dancing and rapping outside the Oakland Baseball Stadium. He made tapes which he sold to people entering the stadium to see the Oakland A's play. Many people put contributions into a cardboard box as he exhibited his dancing and rapping on the street outside the stadium. His friends came by and laughed at him. "Man, you can't dance. You can't rap! Why don't you go and get you a real job and stop all this foolishness?" He told them he believed he could rap and could dance and that he had a dream. A dream? They laughed in his face.

Well, guess who's laughing now. Mr. Stanley Kirk Burrell, otherwise known as Hammer, is listed on Forbes Top 100 as one of the wealthiest entertainers in the world. He has sold more records than any other rap artist in history, and he recently built a $20 million home, which has all the modern amenities, even a bowling alley. Many of those same friends who used to laugh at him are now working for his company as hourly wage employees. Do not, I repeat, do not listen to, hang out with, associate with people who like to use the word "Can't." They will kill your dreams.

• • • • • • • • • •▬▬▬▬▬• • • • • • • •

THE MAN IN THE MIRROR

"You can't do that." "You just don't have what it takes."
"You're not good enough." These statements are common
tools of dreambusters. They are frequently associated with
people who talk us out of our best ideas and biggest
dreams. The problem is that the main person who makes
these statements is the person we see every day in the
mirror, it is us! Many of us are our own worst enemies. We
talk ourselves out of our best dreams and ideas, by telling
ourselves "We can't do it," "We don't have what it takes,"
"We are not good enough"! We all have experienced times
when we have doubted ourselves, and have doubted our
abilities and therefore squelched what could have been
very profitable and productive activities, simply because we
didn't think we could. Well, I've said it before and I'll keep
saying it. If you can control the enemy on the inside, the
enemy on the outside cannot do you any harm. In reaching
our potential, we must always start with self. First we must
work on our own self-image. We must develop an "I can
and I will" attitude and eliminate all negative self-talk as
soon as it starts to enter our minds. Talk to yourself and tell
yourself, "I can, oh yes I can." Greet yourself in the mirror
every day and say to yourself, "You are one of the greatest
people the world has ever known and you are going to do
unbelievable things today." Start with the person in the mirror, then you can begin to change those outside the mirror!

Each time you achieve something, even small things, you are in essence adding to your self esteem, your self image, your self concept. You are subconsciously saying, "I'm all right and I can do it." And you have to ignore anyone who says "You can't," even if it is you!

FEAR NOT

Today I want to share a quote with you from the book *Success Is Never Ending and Failure Is Never Final,* by Dr. Robert Schuller. "Fear not that you might make a mistake believing in your dream. Fear rather that if you don't go for it you might stand before God and he'll tell you that you could have succeeded if you had just had more faith.

"Fear not that you might fail. Fear rather that you will never succeed, if you never try and are unwilling to take risks. Fear not that you might be hurt. Fear rather that you might never grow if you wait for painless success."

Friends, fear not, but rather dare to dream. The old man said to the young man when comforting him on his fears, "Why not go out on a limb? Isn't that where the fruit is?" It is impossible to reach second base if you are afraid to leave first base. You've got to have a dream and then dare to act on that dream, in order to achieve that dream!

A DREAM, THEN A DO!

We've been talking about dreams and goals and how they are the seeds for success. They are the starting point for success. But once you have your dreams you need to learn how to actualize them, how to make them into realities. Well, after you dream, you must learn to do. First you need a dream, then you need a "Do." You need to do something about your dreams; you need to go after your dreams. You have to pursue your dreams. You must go for it and not "forgo" it. To make your dreams come true you must do something, because faith without works is really no faith at all.

Dreams are the seeds for success. To make your dreams come true you must move on them, take action on them, pursue them, go after them. Otherwise they are simply pipe dreams or wishes, which have no substance. A dream mixed with confidence, determination, persistence, strong desire and action cannot be denied!

JESSE OWENS, A DREAMER!

A dream mixed with confidence, determination, persistence and strong faith is destined to become a reality. The bigger the dream, the bigger the rewards. Jesse Owens was a world-class athlete who was told that because he was black, there was no way he could compete on the same level as the Aryan athletes of Nazi Germany. Hitler came to the games but refused to greet this black athlete from the United States. What Hitler did not know was that Jesse Owens was a skilled athlete who had prepared himself. More importantly, he was armed with a dream and great faith. The 1936 Olympics were held in Berlin, and the Nazi athletes were cheered while Jesse Owens and the American athletes were booed. Jesse did not worry about the boo's or the snub by Hitler, he just concentrated on his dream. He continued to dream even after having a "foot fault" three times. He mixed his dream with his faith and ultimately triumphed, winning four gold medals, one for every event in which he competed. A dream mixed with massive faith, confidence, and determination will always change your destiny!

THE SUN ALWAYS SHINES, BUT . . .

The sun always shines, but some days the clouds cover up
the sunshine. No matter how positive you are, it is important to associate with those who are positive and encourage
you rather than those who are negative. There are two
types of people in life—those who add to you and those
who subtract from you, those who deposit and those who
withdraw. You must decide which ones you want around
you. It's like a bank account, people will either deposit and
add to your dreams or they will subtract and take from
them. If the negative naysayers continue to withdraw from
your dreams then eventually your dreams will come up
"insufficient funds" and the next step is bankruptcy, giving
up on your dreams. Then you start to settle for what life
throws at you instead of determining your own destiny.
Folks, this is not a dress rehearsal! This is it! Follow your
dreams and hang with those who add to your account!

Two Choices?

Today's *Motivational Minute* is taken from the new tape series by James Anthony Carter, "The Unstoppable Visionary." Mr. Carter states, "Creativity and living are not without their difficulties. The unfortunate thing about having a dream is that nobody believes in it initially but you. But when the dream comes true, they'll all say that it was obvious all along! This being the case, you have two choices in life. Listen to the naysayers or follow your dream." Since you are reading this *Motivational Minute*, you have taken a step toward your dream. You have chosen to be different; you have chosen to be yourself. And in choosing to be yourself you have chosen to be that which the creator meant for you to be. Friends, dream big dreams, think big thoughts, because dreams do come true. George Bernard Shaw eloquently said, "Some men see things as they are and ask, why? I dream things that never were and ask, why not?" I ask you to dream big dreams, in fact impossible dreams and continue to ask "Why not?" Remember that all things are possible if you can just believe! Have a great day!

Goals: Stepping Stones To Your Dreams

One of the questions I regularly get is, "What is the difference between dreams and goals?" Well, goals are an out growth of your dreams; they are a direct response to your dreams. A goal is simply a dream with a deadline. Let's say your dream is to go to law school. A goal is when you commit to a time period in which you are going to make this dream into a reality, then you have focused the dream and made it into your goal.

Zig Ziglar has a great analogy where he says that a magnifying glass can ignite a fire on a pile of leaves if you concentrate the power of the sun through the glass at a focused, specific spot and do not move the glass. Goals help to focus your dreams and make you specify WHEN you want to achieve them. They are stepping stones to making your dreams come true. The key is to dream big dreams, think big thoughts, transform those dreams into attainable, reachable goals and then act!

SHARKS

In order to reach your goals, you must be motivated, and there are two types of motivation: inspiration and desperation. Most people usually allow desperation to motivate them. They only get motivated when their backs are up against the wall and they have no other choice. Well, what would happen if we were motivated and gave our all, every day? Let me share this poem by Gary Mattson:

> Most people never learn how fast they can swim
> Until there are sharks pursuing them,
> But the person who succeeds in life's great race
> Is the one who wisely sets the pace.
> Their pace is not set as fear requires;
> Their stroke is a product of their desires.
> As you face oceans of decision,
> Are you guided by fear or by vision?
> Have you set your goals? Are you trying to reach
>   high marks?
> Or are you still waiting to see the sharks?

Folks, let's get motivated every day. Remember, all things are possible if you can just believe! Have a fantastic day!

CALIFORNIA OR BUST!

What is the essential ingredient that propels a person to success? What is the special key that unlocks untold doors? What is the tool that helps mold your future? Well, it's simple yet greatly misused and misunderstood. It is a goal. A goal is a dream with a time frame attached to it. Goals are stepping stones to reach our dreams. If we can concentrate on goals, learn how to set them and how to reach them, we can reach exceptional heights. The pioneers during the California Gold Rush had the goal of reaching California. They had a saying: "California or Bust!" They had a dream, set a time to achieve it and made a commitment to reach their goal or else. We must make the same commitments to reach our goals and then do it!

A GOAL: A TARGET

How do you make your dreams come true? First you have to know what your dreams are. If I gave you a ball and told you to hit a ten-foot wall that was five feet in front of you, could you do it? Of course, no problem! But if I blindfolded you and took you five steps back and then twirled you around ten times would you still be able to hit the wall with ease? No! Because it is difficult to hit what you can't see, and it is impossible to hit what you don't know! That is why you must set goals. The starting point for your goals are your dreams, because a goal is nothing more than a dream with a deadline.

What are your dreams for this year? What are your goals for this year? What do you want to accomplish in the next twelve months? Let's do an exercise to help you to focus on your goals. Take out a piece of paper and number from one to ten. Now I want you to think, what would you go after if you were guaranteed not to fail? What would you attempt, what would you try to accomplish if you were told that it was impossible for you to fail? Think like a child on Christmas morning. Anything you want, you can achieve. Anything. Write down at least 10 things; if you have more, write more. Do not limit yourself by your present circumstances, anything you want you can accomplish; it is now impossible for you to fail.

Once you have made your list you have taken the first step to success. Make copies of that list and read it every day. Read it and reread it until you believe it, then read it some more. Keep on reading it and start acting on it and you will be amazed at how many things you will start to accomplish. If you can dream it you can do it!

THE DREAMSHEET

Yesterday we completed an exercise that would help us determine our dreams and goals, because we realized that it is impossible to hit a target you cannot see and that you do not know. I told you to make a list of at least 10 things you would go after this year if you knew that it was impossible for you to fail. Now that your mind is in the possibility mode, let's go a step further. I want you to take out four sheets of paper. On the first sheet write, "My lifetime dreams and goals." On the second sheet write, "My 12-month dreams and goals." On the third sheet write, "My 30-day goals," and on the fourth sheet write "My successful daily routine."

Once you have developed a routine for a successful day then the key to success is simply to reproduce that successful day seven times and you have a successful week, then reproduce that successful week four times and you have a successful month, and reproduce that successful month 12 times and you have a successful year, and you are on your way to creating a successful lifetime. But it all starts with a dream and a goal. Do this exercise right now, and don't limit your dreams by your present circumstances. Remember, you are guaranteed success; it is impossible for you to fail!

Don't Change Your Decision, Change Your Direction!

You've got your dream, you've set your goal, you're ready to get started and then you encounter difficulty. Don't change your decision to go, just change your path to get there! There are numerous paths which lead to each goal. If you're on your way to work and you come to a street that is closed, do you give up and go back home? No! You find another street that's open or another way to get to work. If you encounter difficulty with your goal, don't change your decision to go! Change your direction to get there!

Not long ago, while stuck in a small town due to weather, I was flipping channels and happened upon a documentary on the great martial arts sensation Bruce Lee. I was extremely interested in him because I remembered as a child how much I liked his character, Kato, in the Green Hornet television show. I sat up and looked at the documentary and was highly impressed with the information I learned. Bruce Lee was born in San Francisco but his family moved back to China while he was a small child. He grew up learning martial arts and acting and found a way to combine his two loves into a unique artistic expression. He came back to America and began to teach his new artistic form of karate. During his struggling days he wrote a "major aim" sheet, which detailed his lifetime goals and dreams. His biggest goal was to be the highest paid and best known Asian actor and martial artist of all time.

He struggled for a while after the cancellation of the Green Hornet and soon went back to China where he began making martial arts movies. The movies became hits and he was a major success in China. The same producers and movie makers who had turned him down in America were now calling and making him offers. He was such a big star everywhere else that he was able to leverage his popularity into a contract that made him the highest paid Asian artist of all times! Shortly after finishing "Enter The Dragon" he died from hypersensitivity to a pain reliever. Yet he had reached his goal, his "major aim." His fame continued after his death with a hit movie and a star on the Hollywood Walk Of Fame.

The main point of this story is that life is very unpredictable. There is little to depend on except your dreams and your faith. If you can set goals, or in this case "major aims," and have the guts to go after those dreams, then you can do incredible things. As Bruce Lee proved, dreams do come true! Dream big dreams, think big thoughts and make sure to write them down and read them at least twice per day and you too can make your dreams come true. Remember all things are possible if you can just believe. Have a great day!

As a Man Thinketh, So As He Is!

"**S**o as a man thinketh in his heart, so as he is" (Proverbs 23:7). For many years I had heard that verse, without it having much effect on me. I thought in life you just were supposed to go with the flow and what happened, or did not happen, was just the way it was meant to be. And those who were successful were just lucky. I went with the flow, and most times I was like a ship lost in the storm, just getting tossed from here to there and from there to here and constantly lost. Then I started to realize I had some personal responsibility for my success and that my thinking determined my actions. I reread the verse over and over and came to see that it is not just my thinking , but my thinking in my heart, my true, core beliefs, that determine what I am and therefore what I will do.

When we deal with our true beliefs we are not just talking about what we are thinking in our head but also what we believe in our heart. Why does it say, "as he thinketh in his heart"? Well, what we think in our head can be quite different from what we think in our hearts. Motivation deals with our heads; its job is to get us to take action, to get up and do something. Inspiration deals with our hearts, the inner person, and it really does not care what our heads have to say. The head may say that what we plan to do is illogical, impossible, and cannot be done. But the heart does not care and ignores the head and the logic of the issue and goes after what it feels it must go after. We have heard countless times of people who were inspired to achieve impossible results—athletes who dedicate a game to a fallen friend or family member and do things that they never thought they could do. Or stories of people who are in accidents or disasters who exhibit superhuman strength to rescue others. As people thinketh in their heart, so as they are!

THE REAL YOU

When you look in the mirror, you see a face you have known all of your life. You see a person that you intimately connect to, you see you. But it is not the real you, the true you. The real you is on the inside, the inner person. And that inner person is directly responsible for the outer you and things you do or don't do. As a man thinketh in his heart, his core, his true being, so as he is! The inner you is the core you. Just as the heart of the artichoke is the prime part, the best part. The core of the apple is the most important part because after all is said and done (or in this case, after all is peeled and eaten), the core contains the seed which is the future of the apple. (If you cut an apple in half you could count the seeds in that apple, but you could not count the potential apples that are in those seeds!)

The center of the pineapple is where the sweetest fruit is found. The same is true for us. The heart is the core, where our most intense thoughts, feelings and beliefs are found. If you can tap the inner person and tap the thoughts and feelings found there, you can begin to tap into your true thoughts, dreams, beliefs and values. These are the things which make you act on your desires. These are the things that guide, direct and determine how you live your life. This is where you determine what you will and will not do. What you go after and what you choose to ignore, what you attempt and what you shy away from. As a man thinketh in his heart, in his core, his inner man, so as he is. The core, the center, the heart is the real you!

CHANGE YOUR THINKING

To change where you're going you must first change your thinking. Your thinking effects how you act and therefore what you do. Just as to change your weight and health you must change what you eat. The same is true for your mind. You must fill your mind with positive, healthy, inspirational and encouraging material and get rid of the things that will kill your dreams and aspirations: doubt, fear and negative thinking. Change your thinking and change your life!

YOU CAN LEAD A HORSE TO WATER, BUT . . .

You can lead a horse to water, but you can't make him drink. You can take a fool to wisdom, but can't make him think. There is a story about a man who was looking for the secret to success. He came to a wise man and asked, "What do I have to do to become a success?" The wise man said, "You have to change your thinking and change what you do and change how you act and finally you have to be willing to make some sacrifices." The young man walked away because he didn't want to change his thinking and didn't want to stop doing what he was doing. He didn't want to make the necessary sacrifices because it would be uncomfortable.

Many have heard what it takes to be successful but refuse to change and therefore choose to fail. Ladies and gentlemen, it's as old as time. You are what you think about. Change your thinking and change your life!

We become what we think about. How you think determines what you do and what goals you will go after. Those who think about a definite goal are more likely to reach that goal, while those who think about nothing tend to do nothing. Those who have no idea where they are going have thoughts of confusion, doubt and fear. Since that is what they think about, that is usually what they get—lives filled with confusion, anxiety and doubt. If you think about nothing you tend to do nothing; if you think about great things you are more apt to do great things!

THE POISON MUSHROOM

Earl Nightengale said, "To become a success you must be careful what you allow to enter your mind, because your mind is like a garden. It will grow whatever is planted." If you plant positive it will grow positive, but if you plant negative you will grow negative. If you plant corn it will grow corn, but if you plant poison mushrooms, they too will grow. That is why you must be careful what you allow to enter your mind, for whatever enters the mind will grow. As you sow so shall you reap. Think about nothing and you will do nothing: think about great things and you will do great things!

MAKE IT A WINNING LIFE

Every day is a great day, and even if it doesn't feel like a great day you can make it a great day. My friend, Wolf Rinke, author of *Make It A Winning Life: Success Strategies For Life, Love And Business,* says that life is essentially what you make it and that you must make things happen for yourself. You make every day a great day by programming your mind that it is a great day! Psychiatrists say that most illnesses are psychosomatic, which means your mind creates them. We all know people who, no matter what kind of illness you might mention, have either had it or are having it! There is a definite relationship between the psyche, which is your mind, and the soma, which is your body. Just as your mind creates the illness in your body, studies show that if you program your mind with positive rather than negative information it can create an exhilarating and exceptional day, every day. Every day can be a great day and your life can be a winning life if you are willing to make it that way. Think great thoughts, do great things and make it a winning day and a winning life!

INSANITY?

To change where you are, you must change your thinking. Your thinking not only determines where you are today but, more importantly, where you are going tomorrow. If you want success it is imperative that you change your thinking, because the definition of insanity is to keep on doing exactly what you've been doing the exact same way and expect different results! You've got to change your thinking, because if you can change how you think you will change how you act; and if you can change how you act you will change what you do; and if you can change what you do then you will change what you get; and if you can change what you get you will change where you're going; and if you can change where you're going you will change your life! Change your thinking and change your life!

Go With The Flow?

"If it is to be, then it is up to me." We've all heard this saying but what does it really mean? Well, it means we must take responsibility for our success or our failure. We either act on life or life will act on us; we can either go with the flow, which may take us any old place, or we can direct the flow and therefore determine our destination. If you look at boats sailing on the river you will notice that if the wind is blowing from the south, many boats will go with the flow, and travel north. But there will also be boats traveling south, east and west. They are not going with the flow but rather are using the flow to go where they really want to go! You determine where you want to go in life. It may not be easy to go where there is no path, but if you do, you'll be the trailblazer!

Your thinking determines how you act and what you do, which determines what you get, and what you get determines where you go. It sounds so simple, yet I often wonder why I didn't change my thinking earlier. Since I was able to change my thinking, why don't others simply change theirs. The reason is that even though it sounds simple, it is not. I once heard someone say, "You are where you are and what you are because of what goes into your mind, which creates your thinking." The traditional way of thinking is to go with the flow and just take whatever life gives you.

When I was a full-time musician, one of my friends told me to "go with flow, go with what's going good." It sounded so cool and hip I accepted it as my philosophy, even though what was "going good" may not have been what I really wanted to do or where I really wanted to go. In fact, what I thought was living well was really a mirage. I was so far behind that I thought I was in front!

For example, I was offered a job I really did not want, but I figured, "Go with what's going, go with the flow" (even though it wasn't where I really wanted to go). I hated the job and it literally made me sick, but I stayed because it kept paying me. I now realize how backward that thinking was; in fact it is the way many people think. Statistics show that over 80 percent of Americans go to jobs they really cannot stand. I know it's true because I was one of them, a backward thinker. You could say the way I was thinking was so backward that if you took my brain and put it in a bird, that bird would take off and fly backward!

Once I changed my thinking, I started to read about others who had decided to do what they wanted to do and to use the flow to go where they wanted to go. I read about others who realized you must change your thinking in order to change your life, otherwise you remain the same, at the same place, doing the same thing and getting the same results. As Zig Ziglar says, "You gotta change that stinking thinking!"

THE SMALL-MINDED
FISHERMAN

To have big achievements you must have big
dreams and big goals. You should never settle for your
present circumstances; instead, you should always
reach higher. There is a story about a fisherman who
caught fish with such ease that it was amazing. But
after catching the fish he did something strange.
He kept the little ones and threw the big ones back.
Someone asked him why he did this, and he an-
swered that it was because he only had a little pan!
Ladies and gentlemen, our reach should always exceed our grasp!

THE CREATIVE-THINKING
FISHERMAN

We talked about how many people let their circumstances and their situations limit what they think they
can achieve. I shared the story about the short-sighted
fisherman who kept the little fish and threw the big
ones back, because he had a little pan. Well, to go one
step further, not only was he short sighted, but due
to his limited vision and lack of imagination, he was
unable to take advantage of obvious opportunities. His
vision was so limited that he could not think of any
other options to reach his goal. The problem was not
the size of the pan but rather the size of his thinking.
Little thinking always limits possibilities. He could have
simply cut the fish into smaller pieces, rather than
throwing the fish back. Too many of us let our present
circumstances stop us and shackle our creativity. To
make your dreams come true you must be creative and
allow you mind to soar, as it was meant to do. Remember, you can if you think you can!

THE OLE COUNTRY DOG

Most people don't live their dreams because they are afraid and they don't want to take any chances. They would rather sit around, complain and bemoan their state, than to live their dreams. They let life determine where they are going. Like the old saying, "If you don't know where you're going, any road will do." If you don't know who you are, you'll answer to any name and any name will do. Did you know that the number one time for people to have heart attacks is between 7 and 9 o'clock on Monday mornings? The time when people have to get up and go to jobs that they hate. Jobs they can't stand. And then they sit around and complain all day long!

Well, ladies and gentlemen, you should never complain about what you allow. You *do* have a choice. I'll share a story that illustrates this point. There was a man walking down a country road. He walked past a porch, where an old farmer was sitting in his rocking chair, and next to him was a dog just howling and making all sorts of noise. So the man walked up to the farmer and said, "Why is the dog howling and making so much noise?" The farmer said, "Because he's sitting on a nail.", and the man said, "Why doesn't he get up?" and the farmer replied, "cause it don't hurt bad enough!" If you go to a job you can't stand and all you do is sit around and complain, then you're no better than that old dog sitting on a nail. Ladies and gentlemen, don't complain about what you allow. You have a choice; you should choose where you go in life. You can, if you want to! Choose to be great!

GROWING PAINS

Most people don't live life to the fullest because they have fear. They let fear rob them of life and let it take time away from them. I don't want you to be reckless and foolish, but I do want you to take chances and challenge yourself, because if you're afraid to take some risk you will never grow, never stretch, never reach your potential. It's impossible to reach second base if you're afraid to leave first. You've got to be willing to stretch, to grow, to push yourself, to go for it and not forgo it. And sometimes it will be painful, but there is no growth without pain. That's why they call them growing pains.

What would you think if you had a baby who was three years old and had not grown from infancy? You'd rush it to the doctor. Or if the baby fell down once and just stopped trying, you'd say there was something wrong, for you know that without falling and getting back up the baby would never learn to walk!

We cannot stop trying just because we fall a few times or just because it is painful. Growth is painful but it is necessary. This is a quote from the families of the astronauts, who died in the tragic Challenger space flight: "Do not fear risk; all exploration, all growth is calculated. Life is filled with challenge. Only those who are willing to go after those challenges grow. Only if we are willing to walk over the edge can we become winners." Remember that all things are possible if you can just believe!

YES I CAN!

If you want to be successful, if you want to make
your dreams into realities, then you have to change
your thinking. You have to develop your thinking
to the point where you honestly believe it is impossible
for you to fail. A few years ago there was a great football game between the Houston Oilers and the Buffalo
Bills. The Houston Oilers were ahead at halftime, 35 to
3. Buffalo had its second string quarterback in and
everybody was just hoping the game would end soon
to put the Bills out of their misery. But the Bills didn't
doubt their ability or that they could win the game!
They came out the second half and scored 38 points
to win the game 41 to 38! This is a clear example that
to be a winner you must think like a winner.

I want to share a poem I received from a friend, Rhonda Davis Smith, the communication expert.

> If you think you are beaten you are,
> If you think you dare not, you don't.
> If you like to win but you think you can't,
> It's almost a cinch you won't.
> If you think you'll lose, you've lost,
> For in this world you will surely find
> Success being with a person's will,
> It's all in the state of mind.
> Think big and your deeds will grow,
> Think small and you'll fall behind.
> Think that you can and you will,
> It's all in the state of mind.
> If you think you're outclassed you are,
> You have to think big to rise.
> You've got to be sure of yourself
> Before you can win the prize.
> Life's battles don't always go
> To the strongest woman or man,
> But sooner or later the person who wins
> Is the person who thinks they can.

You Can, If You Think You Can!

This is a piece I received from the staff at WKYS Radio in Washington, DC who sent this to friends and loved ones to help brighten their day. I hope it helps to brighten yours.

You can be a total winner, even if you're a
  beginner,
If you think you can, you can.
You can take a C up to an A
You can get in the school play, if you think
  you can.
You can wear the gold medallion
You can ride your black stallion, if you think
  you can.
It's not your talent or the gift at birth,
It's not your bank book that determines worth
And it isn't in your sex or the color of your skin
It's your attitude that lets you win.
You can profit through deflation,
Redirect this nation, if you think you can, you
  can.
It doesn't matter if you've won before,
What's the difference what's the half-time score?
It's never over till the final gun . . . Is there one?
Keep on trying and you'll find you've won.
You grab a dream, and then believe it,
Go out and serve with value and you'll achieve it,
If you think you can, you can.
If you think you can, you can.

BARGAINED WITH LIFE FOR A PENNY

Another great day! That's right, another great day! It is another great day because you determine whether today
will be great or miserable. You determine whether you will
be a success or a failure. You determine what you get out
of life by what you put into life. Most people receive not and
achieve not because they ask not and believe not. Most
people settle for the leftovers that life gives them rather than
going out and eating from the banquet table of life. This is
a poem that illustrates this point.

> I bargained with life for a penny,
> And life would pay no more,
> However I begged at evening,
> When I counted my scanty store.
> For life is a just employer,
> And gives you what you ask,
> But once you have set the wages,
> Why, then you must bear the task.
> I worked for a menial hire,
> Only to learn dismayed,
> That any wage I had asked life for,
> Life would have gladly paid.

Friends, stop settling for pennies when you can have
dollars. Dream big dreams, think big thoughts and you can
have your hearts desire!

SETTLING FOR THE LEFTOVERS

We talked about how most people settle in life for the leftovers that life gives rather than creating for themselves a banquet table. They dream little dreams, think little thoughts and get little results. Why? Because most don't think they can do any better. They settle for mediocrity rather than going the extra few steps for excellence, because they don't think they can do it. And if you think you can or think you can't, either way you're probably right! You accomplish what you think you can accomplish. You can if you think you can and you probably won't if you think you can't, because most people won't try. They go to their graves with their dreams inside of them because they don't even try. Well, in America there is no excuse for failure. You live in one of the greatest countries that has ever existed. It's a land with unbelievable opportunities, and yet most of us act like the man who was told to go into a bank and take whatever he wanted. He took a few pennies and left because he didn't think he could handle any more! Ladies and gentlemen, we are what we believe we are. If you can dream it you can do it!

* * * * * * * * * * *

IT DOES NOT MATTER
WHERE YOU COME FROM

We talked about the story of the man who went into the bank and was told to take whatever he wanted and he took a couple pennies, because he didn't think he could handle any more. I also said that to be in America and not to take advantage of the opportunities is to be like that man. Did you know that a person from another country has a four times better chance of becoming a millionaire in America than someone who was born here? Why? Because they want it more. Many of them come from countries with limited opportunities, where they might make five dollars a week and they come to America where they can make five dollars an hour and they work two or three or four jobs. Ladies and gentlemen, they do whatever is necessary to make their dreams come true. They come to this country, see all the opportunities and set about making it happen; while many of us are still sitting around crying, whining and complaining. There is no shortage of money. There is only a shortage of ideas and desire. Dream bigger dreams, think bigger thoughts and make it a great day and a greater life!

No Shortage of Millionaires

Millionaire, millionaire, we hear the word often but we have a vague concept about millionaires. I told you that there is no shortage of money in America but rather a shortage of ideas and a shortage of dreams and desire. That still might not strike home until you realize there is no shortage of money. A millionaire is created in America every fifty-eight minutes, every 58 minutes. There is no shortage of money, only a shortage of ideas and a shortage of desire, real desire to go after your dreams. Ladies and gentlemen, we have to go after our dreams and determine in our minds and in our hearts that we will not stop until we reach our goals. Our dreams and goals should always exceed our reach. We must expand our visions of ourselves, broaden how we perceive ourselves; we've got to stretch, leave our comfort zones and make those dreams come true.

* * * * * * * * * *

IF YOU THINK YOU CAN

If you think you can or think you can't . . . you are probably right. That is an old saying but it is a profound one that never loses its truth. I know from personal experience, because I have found that when I think I can I tend to have a much higher success rate then when I think I can't. Why? Because when I think I can I at least will try. When I made up my mind to change my life, I had to make a conscious decision to think I could, that it was possible to change. First I convinced myself I could make a change, then I started preparing myself for my new life. How? I developed a love of reading, a habit of reading more books and specifically self-development/self-help books and biographies. I read about other people and by doing so I reprogrammed my mind. I developed a mind set that said, "If they can do it, then I can do it." It just depended on how badly I wanted it. I started being exposed to other people who had overcome obstacles and had made a conscious effort to overcome their limiting circumstances. I realized I had talents I was not even using, because I didn't think I could. I went from small achievements to bigger achievements then on to bigger and bigger and bigger achievements, because I started not only think that I could, but more important, to actually believe it. And I found it to be true, that all things are possible if you can just believe!

IF THEY CAN,
SO CAN I!

We become whatever we focus on. Throughout history we have seen countless examples of people who have changed their lives and their circumstances by changing their thinking . . . their focus. We have heard of those who have programmed their minds to believe they could, when all around them said that they couldn't. They have developed the faith to overcome impossible situations because they believed it was impossible to fail. Andrew Carnegie, who came to this country poor and uneducated—yet he went on to become the president of one of the largest steel companies in the world; Les Brown, who was born on a floor in an abandoned building, adopted by a single woman, raised on public assistance and labeled Educable Mentally Retarded and destined for failure—but he went on to become one of the top motivational speakers and media personalities in America; Dave Thomas, who was also adopted and given little chance of success, quit high school to cook hamburgers at a fast food restaurant—he then went on to start his own restaurant and name it "Wendy's", after his daughter, which is now one of the largest fast food chains in the world; John H. Johnson, born in a tin roofed house in Arkansas City, Arkansas, lived on welfare as a child, borrowed $500 from his mother to start his publishing company, which many predicted would fail—but he went on to publish *Ebony* magazine and has become one of America's wealthiest entrepreneurs. We are what we think about. Think great and be great, because it does not matter where you come from . . . it only matters where you are going! Have a Great Day!

***

Fly Like A Bumblebee

No fear, no doubt. This is it, look out! Success is an amazing adventure. It is the process of having a dream and then pursuing that dream with your whole heart. It is getting to the point where you believe it is impossible to fail. A few years ago I had the opportunity to meet Mary Kay Ash, the founder and president of Mary Kay Cosmetics. Mary Kay Ash is a remarkable woman who had a dream that others called impossible. She refused to listen to the naysayers, and went on to build a business that is now one of the largest cosmetic companies in the world. The symbol for her company is a bumble bee and it represents the ability to do the impossible. Why? Because scientists have emphatically stated for years that it is impossible for the bumble bee to fly because of its small wings and big body. But the bumble bee doesn't know that, so it flies anyway! Folks, the only one that ultimately keeps you from being great is you, and your limiting beliefs. Stop saying you can't and start saying, "It's impossible for me to fail." And you too will do unbelievable things. Have a great day!

***

HANNIBAL, OVERCOMING THE OBSTACLES

Hannibal was a great African general and statesmen. He overcame great handicaps and accomplished the impossible because he thought he could. He realized the only real limits in life are those we impose on ourselves. Hannibal was from the city of Carthage, whose arch enemies were the Romans. In 220 B.C. A war started between Rome and Carthage. Hannibal's troops were greatly outnumbered and had fewer weapons and supplies than the great Roman army, but Hannibal did not let that keep him from believing he could win and then acting on that belief. He came up with a daring plan to defeat the Romans. He knew he could not win in a frontal attack so he decided to do the impossible, to attack from the rear, over the Alps. But it was said to be impossible because the Alps were impassable. He developed a strategy where his troops would use great African elephants to go over the Alps. These mountains were called uncrossable, yet Hannibal successfully crossed them and conquered the Romans. He went on to become one of the greatest military strategists and leaders of all time. We still repeat one of his classic quotes: "Either find a way . . . Or make a way!" I implore you to go after your dreams, even those that are said to be impossible. If there is no way, make a way! If there is no path, then make one! Whatever you think you can do, you will see it can come true!

The process of changing my thinking was not easy, but I realized I was not living up to my potential, there was more I could do and it was up to me to do it. I had waited long enough for life to drop success in my lap and it had not happened. I had been living as though I had a thousand years to live. The average life expectancy is 70 years old, if you are currently 18 then you have approximately 700 months to live. If you are 30 then you have 500 months until you are 70, if 40 then you have 375 months until 70, if 50 then you have 250 months to 70, and if you are 60 you have 125 months until 70. I realized every minute is precious and that it is up to me to make the most of the time I am here, no matter how much time I have. I heard someone say "What would you regret if you were to die and had not accomplished or tried to accomplish that which you could have done?" I have gone with the flow and I didn't like where the flow was taking me. I was tired of being broke, busted and disgusted and being a prisoner to the circumstances. I decided to make a change. I realized I had to act on life or life would continue to act on me!

SELF DEVELOPMENT

How do you make yourself a better, more productive, more effective person? The key is self development. Just as a body builder goes to the gym to develop his body and to gain strength and power, the same is necessary for development of mind and of your inner strength. You must develop yourself by working on yourself. I do not mean just on the outer self by exercising. That is important, but you must also develop the inner self and develop your mind. Do you develop your mind like your body, maybe by lifting books and encyclopedias? No, the way is to read those books and fill your mind with the information. Fill your mind with the pure, the powerful, the positive and program yourself for success. You can program your mind for success or let it be programmed by others for failure. The key is making the decision to program yourself by reading and filling your mind with information. Create a new you; give yourself a make over, not just for your face and hair, but also for your mind. Read more books and develop a new you!

INVEST IN YOUR MIND

Did you know that the average American reads one book a year while the average self-made millionaire reads one book a month? The average American looks at six hours per day of television while the average self-made millionaire looks at less than two hours of television. To change your thinking it is essential to change what goes into your mind. History proves that readers are leaders because the leaders usually have been the people who read more books! Martin Luther King, Jr., Malcolm X, John H. Johnson, the publisher of *Ebony* Magazine, Mary McLeod Bethune—the list goes on and on. Readers are leaders. Benjamin Franklin once said, "If a man empties his purse into his head, no one can take it away from him. An investment in knowledge always pays the best interest." I implore you to go on a course of self development, read more books and listen to more positive and motivational tapes. And you will then program your mind that your success is possible and your mind will respond in due order.

BREAKING THE MENTAL BARRIERS

If you re-program your mind to see that things are possible,
then your mind will respond to the new information and
go about making those dreams come true. First you must
think it is possible, then you must believe it is possible
and then you must act! Case in point: for years it was said to
be humanly impossible to run a mile in less than four minutes. It couldn't be done! Then in 1954 a young man named
Roger Bannister ignored the common belief and believed
that it was possible. He prepared and eventually ran the mile
in 3 minutes and 59 seconds. He broke the time barrier as
well as the mental barrier. In 1964 a young high school run-
ner named Jim Ryun ran a mile in less than four minutes,
and now even teenagers are able to run four-minute miles,
and the records continue to be broken. Why? Because
they realize that it is possible, it can be done. They have a
new mind set and their mind is now released to go after
what was thought to be impossible. If you think you can or
think you can't . . . you are probably right! Re-program your
mind and go after your dreams and I know that you will
start to break some barriers in your life. Have a great day!

ACRES OF DIAMONDS

The grass is always greener on the other side. Or could it be that they take more time and effort on their grass than you? I was recently talking to a friend who was disappointed because he didn't get a position he thought was better than his present position. I shared a true story with him about a farmer in Africa who became enthralled by the diamond trade. He was so anxious to get rich that he decided to sell his farm and go searching for real riches. He sold the farm to the first person who came along and took what-ever the man could give and went to find riches. After many disappointing years without finding any diamonds he finally gave up and threw himself over a cliff. Well, back at the farm, the man who had bought it was walking across a stream one day and saw a big pretty rock. He took it home and placed it on his mantle. A friend came one day from the city and saw the rock and was amazed. He said, "Wow! This is a diamond, probably one of the biggest diamonds I've ever seen! Where did you find it?" The man said, "I found it in the stream, but hey, there are a whole lot of them around here! They're all over the place." The farm became known as "Acres of Diamonds." Friends, there are dia-monds in your own back yard; you have diamonds all around you, in fact there's a diamond inside of you . . . all you have to do is look! The grass can be just as green and even greener on your side!

How badly do you want it? Are you willing to do that which is uncomfortable in order to grow? Are you willing to undertake some difficulty and begin a course of self development in order to stretch? Are you willing to go the extra mile in order to become a new you? Do you want it badly enough to go against traditional thinking and develop a new mind set so that not only do you think you can but you also believe, in your heart of hearts, that you can, and that you will? Think back and remember the story of the little choo choo train moving up the hill against all odds, saying, "I think I can, I think I can, in fact I know I can." You will soon realize that this little story is not just for children, but is for all of us. As we thinketh in our hearts, so as we are!

I'VE GOT A
NEW ATTITUDE

❖

"**N**ew coat, new hat, new ideas as a matter of fact, I'm changing!" Patti Labelle sang about a new attitude, about how she changed her look and changed her direction. It was an outward sign of an inward shift in her way of looking at the world; her perspective changed. Her way of thinking and acting changed; she had a new attitude! Sometimes it takes a new hat, coat, suit or dress, but we must remember that real change comes from the inside out. The way you feel on the inside ultimately determines how you behave on the outside. You may feel good when you change your appearance, but to effect long-lasting change you must also change your inward appearance.

As we improve our state in life we know we must dream big dreams and think big thoughts. We also know we must consciously change our thinking to take on winners' thoughts. And then we must continue on this quest and realize that we must also get a new attitude, a new perspective, a new way of looking at the world, a new mind set. Your attitude is a combination of your thinking, your emotions, your way of viewing events and circumstances around you, and your perspective. Your attitude is what you do and how you respond to the things which occur in your life.

Without question, attitude is a determining factor in your success or your failure. It is a critical ingredient in the results you create in life. Attitude is the key which starts your magnificent machinery and puts it into action. As Dr. Karl Meninger says, "Attitudes are much more important than facts," and he is right. Attitudes make the difference in success or failure.

It's All About Attitude

Your attitude is more important than the facts! Often times we face seemingly insurmountable problems or we have circumstances we cannot change. Well, our attitudes are much more important than the facts. The fact is that Stevie Wonder was born blind, but his attitude was, "So what? I am not going to let that keep me from being great." Mugsy Boges was born short, but his attitude was that he was not going to let his stature limit how far he was going to go. A few years ago he was a number one draft pick in the NBA draft, going before many taller players. Friends, there are certain facts in your life that cannot be changed, but your attitude can overcome those facts and you can go on to do great things!

GREAT DAY

It's another great day. I am excited about today like I am every day. Why? Because it's another great day. Now that sounds like a play on words. There are a number of things we have no control over, like the weather, but we can control our attitude to life and can create great days. A few weeks ago we had a major storm with fierce winds and torrents of rain. I had a speaking engagement, and when I walked in someone said, "Have you ever seen anything like this rain? What do you have to say about this stuff?" I said, "It is a tough rain and a bad storm, but it's a great day." He said, "What, are you crazy?" I said, "No, I'm not crazy. When I woke up this morning I looked outside and I saw the rain and the storm and said, 'Wow, another great day.'" He said, "What?" I said, "That's right, another great day! Why? Because when I woke up and saw the rain I was glad that I could see the rain. See, there are people who made a whole list of things they were going to do today, had meetings planned, things to do and places to go, and they didn't wake up, they can't see the rain. I'm thankful every morning I wake up because I've got another chance, another opportunity to slay some dragons. And because I have that opportunity, it is a great day." Friends, everyday is a great day if you get another shot at life. Enjoy life, live life to the fullest!

THE UNCOMMON THOUGHT CREATES
THE UNCOMMON MAN

To be great it is necessary to think uncommon thoughts, to do uncommon things and to go after uncommon goals. Rolo May, the renowned psychologist and author of *Man's Search For Meaning,* said, "The opposite of courage is not cowardice but rather conformity." People act like everybody else without knowing where they are going and why. We dissolve into the mainstream rather than choosing to be distinct. We tend to go with the flow rather than directing the flow. President Theodore Roosevelt had an uncommon philosophy, which made him great. He said, "I choose not to be a common man. Me, it's my right to be uncommon if I can. I'll seek opportunity, not security. I do not wish to be a kept citizen humbled and dulled by having the state look after me. I want to take the calculated risk, to dream and to build, to fail and to succeed. I'll refuse to live from hand to mouth. I'll prefer the challenges of life to the guaranteed existence, the thrill of fulfillment to the stale calm of Utopia. I will never cower before any master nor bend to any friend. It is my heritage to stand erect, proud and unafraid, to think and act for myself and face the world boldly and say, this I have done." Frank Sinatra sang the song, "I Did It My Way." Folks, I say to you, do it *your* way; think uncommon thoughts, do uncommon things and you will reach your goals in uncommon hours!

You're As Young As You Think You Are

Your attitude is much more important than the facts. I spoke recently to some senior citizens, and one lady said she was depressed because she didn't feel useful anymore. I asked her if she realized that Colonel Sanders didn't start Kentucky Fried Chicken until he was 65, Clara Peller didn't become a TV star until she was in her 80s and George Burns signed a 10-year performance contract and he's in his 90s! Senior citizens around the country are running marathons, opening businesses and doing amazing things. They realize they are all getting older, but their attitude is more important— they would rather wear out than rust out! George Burns likes to say his daily key to success is to get up and look in the obituaries. If his name is not listed, then he gets busy! Enjoy life . . . all of your life!

In most cases attitude is the only thing that actually separates the winners from the losers. I have often seen times when two football teams were equally matched in talent, skill and preparation but possessed different attitudes or states of mind, that state of mind created the difference in the outcome! Attitude is the thin line between success and failure. Attitude is the common denominator among those who are able to rise above their circumstances. It is the key ingredient which sets the winners apart from the losers. Attitude determines whether you stay on track, headed toward your goal, or whether you give in to the day-to-day challenges which can keep you from achieving your potential.

Usually when people speak of "attitude" they refer to a person's disposition, temperament or personality. We all know people who "have an attitude," which usually means a bad attitude. A bad attitude refers not only to a poor disposition but also to a poor mental mind set, a negative way of looking at the world. It is a way to see only the negative aspects of each situation . . . the glass is half empty rather than half full. It's a pessimistic view of the world. I read that the definition of a pessimist is someone who complains about the noise when opportunity knocks!

Well, if there is such a thing as a bad attitude, there must also be such a thing as a good attitude, a positive perspective and an optimistic view. A positive mental attitude creates optimism and positive expectations. As Larry Winget, the motivational speaker says, "No matter what you do in life, you will do it much better with a positive mental attitude than a negative mental attitude."

OPTIMISM

As you develop a positive mental attitude, you will also develop optimism. Optimism is the attitude that expects good things to happen and the ability to believe that positive things are going to result from your actions. If you are optimistic you develop the expectation of seeing the good in things rather than the bad. As you develop your positive mental attitude, remember to remain optimistic. Look for the rainbow but realize you can't have it unless it rains. I like to use a phrase I heard which says, "I'm so optimistic that I am going fishing for Moby Dick in a row boat, and I'm taking the tarter sauce with me."

Statistics show that attitude makes a difference, not only in achievement but also in physical health. People with a positive attitude tend to get sick less and when they are sick, they get well quicker.

EXPECTANCY

In order to be a success, you need to cultivate a positive mental attitude. Everyday you need a positive outlook and a positive expectancy. A positive outlook is to look for the good in situations rather than the bad. A positive outlook is to see the rain and be excited because you know that plants need water and without the rain we would live in a desert. A positive expectancy is to expect great things. It is said that miracles usually come to those who expect them and welcome them. Expect great things and develop a positive mental attitude and you will be able to do great things. With a positive mental attitude you can weather every storm and know that with every blessing there is a burden and with every burden there is a blessing. Have a great day!

MADAM C.J. WALKER

Madam C.J. Walker was a lady who refused to let her initial circumstances keep her from achieving greatness. She was not a highly educated person, but a lady with a great positive mental attitude. Because of her attitude, she was able to rise above those who were more talented and more educated. She was able to reach unbelievable heights and make millions of dollars. Madam C.J. Walker was the first black woman to become a millionaire in America! She realized that it is your attitude not your aptitude that ultimately determines your altitude. Develop a positive mental attitude and you too can rise to the top!

There is a story about two little boys, one was an optimist the other a pessimist. A group of researchers conducted a study on positive and negative mental attitudes and the boys were recruited. First, the researchers took the boy with the negative mental attitude and put him in a room filled with the newest and most exciting toys and video games. There were all sorts of toys and games and machinery that kids around the world had chosen as the absolute best. They left him in the room and told him to have a good time. The second little boy, the optimist, was put into quite a different room. He was placed in a room filled with horse manure!

The researchers observed the boys through two-way mirrors and were quite amazed at their findings. The pessimistic boy just sat in the middle of the room and cried, while the optimistic boy was laughing and smiling and jumping around, having a ball. When the researchers questioned the pessimistic boy, they asked why he was crying amid all the wonderful toys and games. He explained he was afraid to enjoy the toys for he was sure someone would eventually take them or he might break them or that there might be something wrong with the toys! Then they went to the room where the optimistic boy was still jumping around and having a ball, in the midst of the hip-high horse manure. They asked him why he was having such a good time and he replied,

"You can't fool me. With all this horse stuff I know there must be a pony in here somewhere!"

Friends, life is too short to half-way live it! You should decide to live your life to the fullest and cherish every moment. Enjoy life. It is a shame when people commit suicide and throw away their tomorrows. Well, it is also a shame to throw your life away bit by bit and piece by piece by not living up to your potential. Whether you kill yourself fast or slow the end result is still the same—you don't live life to the fullest and therefore miss out on many of its real joys. ALWAYS, LIVE LIFE TO THE FULLEST!

FIND YOUR LIFE'S PURPOSE

I want to share with you today a story I got from Dennis Kimbro, the author of *Think And Grow Rich: A Black Choice.* Dennis told a story about Malcolm X he heard from Percy Sutton, the Manhattan Burrough President. As a young lawyer, Percy Sutton represented Malcolm X in a court case and won against overwhelming odds. It was a very intense court battle between Malcolm and his adversaries. As they were leaving the courthouse, Malcolm's supporters were on one side and his adversaries were on the other. Malcolm and Percy Sutton had to be protected by a number of body-guards as they made their way to a long black limousine. Percy Sutton was so scared he could hardly speak, while Malcolm was as cool as a cucumber. Percy asked him, "Minister Malcolm, how can you be so cool in the face of all this danger, you could lose your life any minute?" Malcolm calmly replied, "I hadn't even noticed any danger. My mind is thinking about other things, things other than my mortality. But the reason I am not worried is because of a story I heard that gave me a new perspective on life."

"Brother Percy, years ago I was told a story about an old Arab worker named Omar who had a dream and saw the face of death. He woke up and ran to his master and asked if he could have the fastest horse so he could escape death. The master gave him the swiftest horse. He rode without stopping for three days, not stopping for food or sleep or provisions. After three days the road branched into seven separate parts. He took the far right but soon changed his mind, and then took the far left but changed again, and he vacillated from road to road until he had one left. He took that road and rode fast and strong." After he rode about 500 yards, the face of death appeared and said, "Omar, Omar, why have you kept me waiting for three days?" Malcolm X turned to Mr. Sutton and said, "The moral of this story is that you can run and you can hide, you can twist and you can turn, but no matter what you do, you can't get out of this life alive." So while you're here you'd better find your life's purpose, live life to the fullest, pursue excellence and live your dream, because you can't get out of this life alive!

HYACINTH MORGAN

I would like to share the story of Hyacinth Morgan, a lady I met last year. Hyacinth came to America at the age of 20 with a sixth grade education. Her English was poor, but her desire to succeed was great. She started working as a housekeeper and began improving her English. After five years of working she had saved enough money to return to her small native island for her two children who were left with her mother. Her island return was greeted with a demand to pay back taxes. The money saved to bring her children to America was now used to pay property taxes. She stayed on the island and worked and saved another three years then brought her kids to America. She began working again as a domestic, and did that for five years while earning her G.E.D. She finally earned it and went to a local community college with the dream of becoming a doctor. But she was told it was not possible because of her limited educational background. Yet again, her desire to succeed was great. She earned straight A's and was eager to go to a school with a pre-med program. But she was rejected by every school in the country because she was too old, now well past 40. But Hyacinth did not give up. She kept pushing until finally the people at Johns Hopkins University, in Baltimore MD, saw her grades and heard her story and accepted her in their pre-med program, on a full scholarship! Friends, this is a true story of inspiration that proves if you can dream it, you can do it! A dream mixed with faith, confidence, determination and persistence cannot be denied. Remember, all things are possible if you can just believe.

THE NO-OPTION PERSON

We talked about how you have to give your all when you want to reach your goal; you have to be completely focused on your goal; you have to become a no-option person! No-option people have no options: they have to make it or else, do or die, all or nothing. When you become that committed, you will make it happen because you have no other choice. There was a general who was taking his troop to a major battle on an a distant shore. As they approached the enemy he saw they were outnumbered, and his troops were afraid because the enemy seemed so big and strong. But the general knew they had the potential to win. After they hit land he saw the fear and how the men were tentative in advancing, so he gave the order to "Burn the boats." They now had no other choices, no other options; they had to win or die! At that moment his troops became energized and fearless, because they had no other options! They fought and gave their all and they won. We have to develop a sink-or-swim, no-option mind set, a do-or-die attitude. We have to make it happen. If you do, if you make that kind of commitment, then your dreams will come true, in fact it must come true . . . because you have no other option!

THE TALKING BIRD

One of my favorite stories is of a rare talking bird that spoke five languages. A man heard about this rare talking bird and set out on a worldwide search for it. After an exhausting search he stopped in a pet store to ask for more information and it was there that he found the bird! He told the owner that he had to go on a short trip, but to please send the bird to his house in two days. When he arrived home in two days he asked his wife if the bird had arrived, and she said yes. He said, "Where is it?" and she said, "In the oven." "What? That was a one-of-a-kind bird that could speak five languages!" and his wife said, "Well, why didn't it speak up?" Most of us are like that bird: we have skills and talents that could change our lives, but we won't speak up and show the world what we've got to offer. Folks, let others know of your skills and talents, let them know that you are unique. Because there is no one exactly like you. No one!

SPEAK UP

If you want something in life, you have to be willing to
speak up and let people know what you want. We talked
about the bird that would not speak up and therefore became someone's dinner. Well, the same is true for most
people—they do not ask. The Bible says, "Ask and you shall
receive." Well, the converse is also applicable: don't ask,
and you probably will not receive. Most people receive not
because they ask not. As my friend Larry Winget of Win
Seminars says, "If you want more out of life, you must ask
more out of life!" Ask and you will receive, don't ask and
you will only get what life wants to throw your way and not
what you want. If you want to G-E-T, then you need to
A-S-K!

After you start to speak up, you must also be concerned about the
inner conversation that we all experience. Our inner conversation is
the conversation that we either think or verbalize to ourselves. This
inner conversation may seem harmless or inconsequential, but it is actually very important because it has great influence on our actions and
helps to determine our direction. Our attitude not only determines our
actions, but it is connected to our inner conversation, which can also
effect what we will and will not do. We must learn to control our inner
conversation.

Now, Shut Up

Have you had days when you didn't want to get out of bed, not because you're sleepy but because you are tired of problems and would rather just go back to bed? Well, everybody has days like that. But the key to overcoming those days is to change your inner conversation, your inner communication. When that communication tells you that you don't have any reason to get up, you have to learn to respond by saying, "Shut up." That is right, just say, "Shut up," and then tell yourself to get up, get going and get busy, because nobody is going to do it for you but you. Depression is usually the result of negative inner conversation. Get up and read or listen to something positive (like the *Motivational Minute*). Whatever you do, wake up, then get up so you can go up. Have a great day!

Reap And Sow

If you want more out of life, then you must put more
into life. It sounds simple. The more you give, the
more you get; the more you sell, the more money you
make; the more seeds you sow, the more plants you
reap. Most people are waiting for their ship to come in,
but they haven't sent any ships out. They want the
plants to grow but they haven't planted any seeds.
Look, the farmer doesn't go out and sow 10 seeds and
expect a 100 plants. No, he plants lots of seeds and
knows that some might not come up but the more he
plants the more he gets. It's as old as time—as you
sow, so shall you reap. That means you've got to get
busy; you've got to make it happen! If you want more
out of life, then you've got to put more into life. Believe
and you can achieve!

THE CREATIVE SHOESHINE MAN

To be a success, you must find imaginative ways to overcome some of the obstacles you will be presented with.
You've got to be creative. There is a great story about a
busy executive rushing as usual from one meeting to
another. As he left his office he was approached by a shoeshine man who said, "Hey man, you've got some crummy
looking shoes. Why don't you let me give you a shine?" The
businessman said, "No . . . I don't have time." And every
block for the next six blocks he was approached about a
shoeshine and gave the same answer, "No . . . I don't have
time for a shoeshine." Well, at the seventh block he walked
past a shoeshine stand and the man was counting 97, 98,
99, 100. "My friend, you look like a busy man, so I apologize for the interruption. But today is my birthday and I
made myself a promise that I would give a free shine to the
100th person who came by my stand and you are the person. Please allow me the opportunity to give you a shine
and honor my promise." So the businessman sat down, and
the shoe shiner went to work polishing diligently and giving
him a terrific shine. In fact, the shoes looked like they were
brand new. As the businessman was preparing to leave he
said, "What is your regular fee?" The shoe shiner said, "Five
dollars." The man gave him a 10 and said "Happy Birthday."
The shoe shiner stood there for a few minutes and then
said, "97, 98, 99 . . ." Friends, this story just simply shows
that we must be creative and use our wits, because many
times it will be all that we have!

Life makes no promises except that it will be challenging. It almost seems like it is part of the bylaws, that life is difficult. Yet I am confident it becomes infinitely more pleasurable and much easier, if you go about your day with a positive rather than a negative attitude.

In going after your dream, you must be creative, you must believe you can achieve and you must have a mind set that will consistently tell you that it is possible and consistently say "Yes I can," "Yes I can," "Yes I can." You need an "I CAN" attitude, a "YES" attitude, an attitude that makes a difference. A NEW ATTITUDE.

Just Gotta Keep Kickin'—Never Give Up!

In everybody's life you know some rain's gonna fall
At everybody's house sometimes trouble will call.
But when trouble stops by you can just sit there and
cry,
Or you can make up your mind you will stand up and fight.

People listen closely to the sound of my voice,
Success in life is never due to chance but to choice.
You choose to go on, to go through the storm,
Or you choose to give up and give in when things start to
go wrong.

It's up to you, whether you win or lose,
If you want to each the top,
You must believe deep in your heart.
Give it your all, everything you've got,
And never, ever, ever, ever stop.

Just gotta keep kicking, keep on moving,
Just gotta keep striving, keep on trying.

I know you can't control which way the winds gonna blow,
But you determine which way your boat's gonna go.
If the wind is blowing to the north,
But the south is your chosen course,
Then you've got to use the flow,
To make it go where you want it to go.

The race in life does not go to the swift or the strong,
But to the one who just keeps moving along.
The one who claims the winner's cup, even when the race
    gets rough,
Is the one who keeps kicking and never gives up!

These are the lyrics to a song I wrote which speaks to the fact that success is a matter of never giving up. It is a statistical event; you've got to keep trying. You've got to persist. After you develop a new attitude, a new mind set, a new determination and a new way of looking at the world then there is still some more that you have to do. You have a dream, you see the goal, you've got a new attitude, you believe it is possible that you really can achieve your goal. Then you start out toward your goal and the problems and the challenges start to appear. Doors are closed in your face, people say "No!" to your ideas. Mountains appear in your way. What do you do now? Do you give up? No!!!

You must make a focused decision to never give up. If you want success and you want to reach your goals then you must decide to never, ever quit; you must decide to persist. Persistence, the process of never giving up, is the direct response of a positive mental attitude. It is the action step that is the key to all success stories.

One of my favorite stories of persistence is the story of W Mitchell. When I started my quest of self development I constantly heard the name of W Mitchell on tapes by Zig Ziglar, Anthony Robbins and many other great speakers of our time. I was intrigued with the inspiring story of persistence and determination of this man who refused to give up, even when the circumstances and obstacles in his life were overwhelming.

A few years ago I met Mitchell and he was as kind and warm to me as though we had known each other for years. We have since become good friends, and I have heard his story told by him, as only he can tell it. It always reminds me that it really doesn't matter what happens to you in life, it only matters what you do about it!

W MITCHELL, "THE MAN WHO WOULD NOT BE DEFEATED!"

W Mitchell is a man who exemplifies overcoming life's obstacles. He is respectfully called "The man who would not be defeated" because he never gives up. Twenty years ago Mitchell was a student who worked part time as a cable car operator in San Francisco. Between school and work, he found time to ride his new Honda motorcycle for recreation. He lived for times when he could get out on his bike and feel the refreshing wind blow on his face. One day while taking a ride, he was approaching an intersection and suddenly saw a truck running a red light. The truck slammed into

Mitchell. He lay on the ground covered by the wrecked pieces of his motorcycle! As Mitchell lay there in agony he smelled gas and realized he was covered with it. Suddenly there was an explosion; the bike went up in flames; the fire spread and soon engulfed Mitchell! He became a human torch and was completely burned from head to toe. He lost his fingers and toes and was left with no resemblance to his former self. He went through months and months of agonizing surgery and rehabilitation, but he never gave up. He finished his education and went on to start a business that soon became very successful. In fact, he was able to purchase a private plane which he piloted. Mitchell's plane became his passion and he spent all of his spare time flying. One evening the plane started experiencing engine problems. He tried to land but lost control and crashed. When he awoke again, he found that now he was paralyzed from the waist down. He sat and looked at himself and saw a burned man who was now paralyzed and forced to live the rest of his life in a wheelchair. Others expected him to give up, but Mitchell refused to. He said, "There used to be 10,000 things that I could do; now there are 9,000." He went on to share his story with others and has become one of the top motivational speakers in the world. He owns homes in Colorado, California and Hawaii and lives life to the fullest. He lives the life that he talks about. It's not what happens to you that counts, it's what you do about it!

NEVER GIVE UP!

So many have asked me what do you do when life throws
you a curve ball, when Murphy's Law comes into play.
You know, "Whatever can go wrong will go wrong." And
it always seems to come at the most inconvenient time.
Someone once said that in life you've either got a problem,
just left a problem, or you're on your way to a problem.
But even with Murphy, the key to your success is not to give
up—just don't give up. This portion of a very popular poem
illustrates the point.

> When things go wrong as they sometimes will,
> When the road you're trudging seems all uphill,
> When the funds are low and the debts are high,
> When you want to smile but you have to sigh,
> When care is pressing you down a bit,
> Rest if you must but don't you quit.
> Life is queer with its twist and turns,
> As every one of us sometimes learns,
> And many a failure turns about,
> When you might have won, if you'd stuck it out.
> Don't give up, though the pace seems slow,
> You might succeed with another blow.

Folks, don't quit no matter what. Make up your mind
that you are never going to give up!

DON'T QUIT!

Stuff happens! That is a part of life. As long as we are blessed to stay on this earth we will have to pay the price of constantly dealing with the obstacles and challenges that life presents. But we can win, if we just persist; never give up!

> Often the goal is nearer than
> It seems to a faint and faltering man.
> Often the struggler has given up,
> When he might have captured the victor's cup.
> And he learned too late when the night slipped
>   down,
> How close he was to the golden crown.
> Success is failure turned inside out,
> The silver tint of the clouds of doubt,
> And you never can tell how close you are,
> It might be near when it seems afar,
> So stick to the fight when you're hardest hit,
> It's when things seem worse that you mustn't
>   quit.

There is an old saying that is very true which says winners never quit and quitters never win. To be great you must be persistent and never, ever give up on your dream! Remember if you can dream it, you can do it. Have a great day!

I have found that the true definition of greatness is when you have ordinary people who do extraordinary things; people who persist and simply refuse to give up. Persistence compensates for every disadvantage and every limitation that would ordinarily keep people from going after their dreams. Persistence is the asset, the action step that turns your dreams into realities. Determination is an attitude, but persistence is an action, the action of never giving up!

PERSISTENCE

If you want your dreams to come true then it is absolutely necessary that you be persistent. Of all the qualities that create winners, the most important is persistence. You have to keep trying, keep trying, keep trying and resolve in your mind that you will never give up. Never! Persistence breaks down resistance. Life is going to say no, people are going to say no, but if you persist, then life will finally have to say yes! It's a law. Just like the law of gravity says that whatever you throw up will come down, the law of averages says if you keep asking long enough you are going to get a yes; it's got to happen! This is a quote from former president, Calvin Coolidge: "Press on. Nothing can take the place of persistence. Talent will not; the world is full of unsuccessful people with talent. Genius will not; unrewarded genius is almost a proverb. Education alone will not; the world is full of educated derelicts. Persistence and determination alone are omnipotent." As I like to say in my seminars, "You've got to knock and knock and knock and knock and knock—until you knock it open or you knock it down."

THE FEAR OF FAILURE

One of the biggest problems which keeps people from going after their dreams is a fear of failure. Most people are afraid of failure yet they do not realize that failure is a part of success! Every successful person has had some failure, but they use the failure, learn from the failure. They make failure their teacher, not their undertaker. In his quest to invent the light bulb Thomas Edison failed over 10,000 times but he refused to give up. When asked why he did not give up, he said, "I didn't fail. I just discovered another way not to invent the light bulb." William Shakespeare once said, "Our doubts are traitor, and make us lose the good we oft might win, by fearing to attempt." Don't be afraid to fail. In fact, look forward to failure, because if you fail and learn from your failure you are essentially closer to your goal. There was a story about a man who failed in business at the age of 21; was defeated in a legislative race at age 22; and failed again in business at age 24. His sweetheart died when he was 26; had a nervous breakdown at age 27; lost a congressional race at age 34; lost another one at 36; lost a senatorial race at age 45; failed in his effort to become Vice President at age 47; lost a senatorial race at age 49; and at age 52 was elected President of the United States! His name was Abraham Lincoln! Folks, you can never give up. Don't let failure get you down; it's a part of success. Learn from your failures. Make failure your teacher, not your undertaker!

THE STORY OF THE TWO FROGS

You've got to be creative and use all of your talents to overcome your obstacles. We must look for the opportunities in life, and if there are no opportunities we must make some. We must take the lemons that are thrown at us and the ice that people throw on our ideas and make them into lemonade. We've got to believe in ourselves and never give up. This reminds me of a story about two frogs. The first one was hopping along and fell into a bucket of milk. He looked around, got angry, cursed life and its bad breaks and soon gave up and died. The second frog also fell into a bucket of milk, but he had a different attitude, a different perspective, a positive perspective. He didn't like the fact that he fell into the milk, but he directed his energies to the solution rather than just the problem and how unfair it was. He kept on hopping and kept on kicking; he didn't give up. He kicked and he kicked until he churned the milk into butter and was able to hop out! Friends, life is not going to play fair. There will be times when life throws you some curve balls. And your ultimate success or failure will depend on whether you sit around angry at life, concentrating on the problem and how unfair it is, or whether you concentrate on the solution to the problem. I have found, without a doubt, that the key to success is not what happens to you but what you *do* with what happens to you!

Of all the qualities that ultimately make a difference in the quest for success, persistence is definitely the key to achieving your goals. Imagine that you were out last night and did not eat dinner because you were just too busy. When you finally got home, you were too tired to eat so you just fell into bed. The next morning you woke up with severe hunger pains; your stomach was growling and making all kinds of noises. You were starving. You went to the kitchen and opened the refrigerator and it was wiped out, absolutely nothing there. You then went to the cabinet and opened it up, and it was completely empty, not even a cracker! Your stomach was growling, you were starving and you had no food. You had to get something to eat. What are you going to do? Are you going to go to the store? To 7-11? To McDonald's? To a friend's house? What are you going to do?

You run and wash your face and throw on some clothes. You race to the grocery store, but there's a sign on the door that says, "There is a problem with the heating system and the store is temporarily closed." You run down the street to the 7-11. The doors are locked and a sign says the employees are on strike and there are no replacements until later that day. You run frantically to McDonald's and it's closed because the water pipes broke. You are starving. What are you going to do now? Are you going to go to a friend's house, to a restaurant or to another grocery store? Folks, I submit to you that not one person, not one person will say, "I'm gonna give up." You don't even think it! Why? Because when you are hungry, when you are in dire need of food, you keep going until you are fed!

Well, the same is true for your success. You must keep going after your dreams; you must persist. You can never, ever give up! No matter how many doors are slammed in your face, no matter how many mountains and obstacles you encounter, you must develop a no-quit attitude. Never give up, never quit. Persist!

If you look at an ant you will see that it is an incredible creature because it never gives up. If you see an ant going along its way and you put a stick or a brick or anything else in its way, it will then climb over it, go under it, go around it or do whatever is necessary to get to its goal. It never stops, it never gives up. It keeps trying, keeps moving, keeps going after its goal. In fact the only time an ant stops trying is when it dies. Not only does an ant never give up, but it is always preparing for the winter. It works diligently to prepare for the hard times that will come (because sooner or later they will come).

We should all take a lesson from the ant. We should work diligently every day; be committed to setting goals and going after them. We should never give up! No matter what obstacles are thrown in our way, no matter what problems beset us or what circumstances we find ourselves in, we must never give up. We've got to keep going after our dreams and striving to reach our goals. And we must always prepare for the future, put something away for a rainy day. Because just as there is sunshine there will be rain, and just as summer comes so will winter. Work hard, prepare for the difficult times and most of all . . . NEVER GIVE UP!

IMPORTUNITY = PERSISTENCE

I'd like to share one of my favorite stories about persistence. It comes from the 11th chapter of the book of Luke, where Jesus shares this parable. "Suppose you went to a friend's house at midnight, wanting to borrow three loaves of bread. You would shout up to him, a friend of mine has just arrived for a visit and I've nothing to give him to eat." He would call down from his bedroom, "Please don't ask me to get up. The door is locked for the night, and we are all in bed. I can't help you at this time." But I'll tell you this, "Though he won't do it as a friend, if you keep knocking long enough he will get up and give you everything you want, just because of your importunity (persistence)."

IMANI MEANS FAITH!

---

he African culture calls it Imani, the Jewish culture calls it Emunah, the Muslims call it Imam, but whatever you call it, it still means the same thing—faith. Faith is the substance of things hoped for, the evidence of things not seen. It is the belief in someone greater than yourself, and then the action of stepping out on that belief. Faith is taking a thought and then seeing it transformed into a belief, and then seeing the belief transformed to a concrete understanding, a knowledge. That knowledge continues to grow and continues to be transformed until the time that you know, that your "know" knows!

Faith is the understanding that there is a creator who empowers, enlightens, encourages and sustains us, in the sunshine or through the storm. And even with faith, it only takes a minute to change your life!

Two thieves are on the cross and they look across to the great teacher from Nazareth, named Jesus, who was being crucified for teaching a new message to the people of Israel. One shouts out, "So you say that you're the Messiah. Well, since you're the Messiah, why don't you come down from that cross and save yourself, and us too while you're at it?" But the other thief says, "Why don't you be quiet, you fool, don't you realize who you're talking to?" Then he turns to Jesus, the Christ, and says, "Jesus, please remember me when you come into your kingdom." And Jesus replies, "Today you will be with me in paradise, this is my solemn promise." (Luke 23:39-43) *The Living Bible.*

This was a defining moment, for in just a minute a thief made a life-changing request. In that minute his life was changed for eternity. It only took a minute to change his life because he believed there was a force greater than himself that could change his life. Because of his faith he opened his mouth and asked a question that changed his life!

A-S-K

In order to make your dreams come true, many times you will need assistance. You will need help from someone else. Often the person who can help is not far away; is in fact within your grasp. But many people never ask for that assistance. They have such a fear of rejection and so much misplaced pride, they refuse to ask for assistance. There are numerous people who are ready and willing to give help, but no one asks them. It's like the high school beauty queen who almost went to the prom alone because she did not have a date. Finally, the class bookworm asked and she went to the prom with him. The other guys were afraid to ask because they assumed she had many requests and would reject their invitations. The little bookworm felt he had absolutely nothing to lose, so he asked. He asked and he became the big man on campus, not only because he escorted the beauty queen but also because he had the guts to ask. Eventually he became her regular date and then her husband. If you want something out of life, you must be willing to A-S-K. Have faith, believe in yourself and then be willing to act on that belief. Someone else is out there who will believe in you too, and will support your dreams. Ask and you shall receive! Seek and you shall find! If you want to G-E-T you must A-S-K. And remember that all things are possible if you can just believe.

ASK and it shall be given you; SEEK and you shall find; KNOCK and it shall be opened unto you. For everyone who asks receives and he that seeks finds and to him that knocks it shall be opened. As you believe, so shall it be done unto you! If you will take a second and look closely at these scriptures you will always find an action command that relates to the benefit you will receive. Ask, and you shall receive; seek, and you shall find; knock . . . and the door will opened unto you.

In each of these statements there is an action command, something we have to do in order for the second part of the statement to become a reality. We must take some action, display some faith, some belief that it is possible, in order to experience the fullness and rich blessing that we are capable of receiving.

Sometimes after you have set your goals, you've dreamed big dreams, you've done everything that all of the motivational books advised you to do, then life throws you a curve ball. Something happens that is not in the plans and it is something you have no control over. Some people call it "Murphy" and others see it as a part of life. In the book "The Road Less Traveled," by M. Scott Peck, the first line really hits it on the head: "Life is difficult." Life does not play fair, and sometimes life doesn't seem to care. It will throw things at you that will disrupt and distract, that will throw you off track. When you have done all you can think of and are faced with situations that you cannot explain, contain or control, then what do you do?

Those are the times you need to muster up the inner strength that will help you to overcome those obstacles, the inner strength that is a direct result of your faith. It is the faith in God that sustains and holds you when all else has let you down, when all else is insufficient. It is the faith that gives you the assurance that through it all, not only will you survive but you will thrive, and everything will be all right. I'm not talking about a faith that is just a placebo, one that simply pacifies you; I am talking about the deep faith that gives you the will to fight, the faith that gives you the guts to go on. It is the faith that inspires you to rise above your circumstances and to go on, in spite of the difficulties.

———————————◈———————————

DON'T FAINT

I have found that we all experience times when our faith
is tested by the challenges of life. There are times when
we have nothing else to hold on to but our faith. I was talking to a friend who called because she was going through a
physical challenge and found that she had to have a serious
operation. A few days after finding out about her condition
she was hit with another blow. Her 10-year-old son was diagnosed with a life-threatening disease that would leave him
with a permanent heart condition. Her fears for herself soon
dissipated and she was only concerned with his condition.
She called and asked, "Why me?" I shared with her that life is
not fair and it is by its nature difficult and it is most difficult
when the problem is something that you cannot control.
Those are the times when you need faith and you must be
committed to that faith. I like to use the analogy that faith is
like getting into a boat and making a commitment to stay in
the boat, no matter what. If the boat hits rough waters, you
must stay in the boat. If the boat starts to rock, you must
stay in the boat. If the boat turns over, stay in the boat, even
if it sinks . . . stay in the boat! Why? Because you will see
that even though the boat has taken on water, you will be
sustained in the midst of the storm. The scriptures state
that "They that wait on the Lord shall renew their strength.
They shall mount on wings as eagles, they shall run and
not be weary, they shall walk and not faint!" Friends, life has
rough moments and storms will arise, but if you can wait,
and have faith, you will be sustained.

WORK HARD, WORK SMART, TRUST GOD

We've talked about hard work, the need to be diligent and committed to our goals and not to rely on luck, which is by definition when opportunity meets preparation. Success comes from hard work. But it is also very important to work smart, to think about what you're doing, to plan and be organized so you can maximize the benefits that come from your efforts. Then remember that the most important ingredient is to trust God. Even when you feel you're prepared and ready for success, life will try to throw you some curves, knock you down, disrupt, distract, and throw you off track. But just keep in mind that if God is for you, He's greater than the whole world against you, and with faith, deep-rooted faith, it becomes impossible to fail. We have to go after our dreams. Work hard, work smart, and trust God.

Hard Work Works

I received a call from a friend who said she liked the Motivational Minute and wanted to share a saying she got from her mother that helped her reach her goals. That message is "Hard work, works." There is no substitute for hard work. Hard work is to success what wet is to water, hot is to fire, they are inextricably connected. Success is not the result of luck or good fortune, but rather hard work. I heard someone say once that "I am a great believer in luck; the harder I work the more I have of it." In Proverbs it says that hard work brings prosperity, playing around brings poverty. Work hard and remember, all things are possible if you can just believe.

Faith is not a new concept, but for years very few realized that it could be connected to success. Most limited the concept of faith only to spiritual enrichment. It was not thought of as a way to run a business or as a success system. Faith was not thought of as a way to go beyond simply striving and surviving, to actually thriving. In this century a new way of thinking emerged that saw faith as a way not only to increase your spiritual wealth and prosperity but also your physical wealth and prosperity. It was made popular through the work of ministers like Dr. Norman Vincent Peale and then expanded upon by people like Dr. Robert Schuller, Kenneth Copeland and Dr. Frederick K.C. Price.

In "The Power of Positive Thinking," Dr. Norman Vincent Peale showed us that the use of a positive mental attitude, a proper state of mind, induced by simple prayer, could produce spiritual and material success on earth. Dr. Peale stressed a simple yet meaningful message that was not a "Pie in the sky" ideology but a theology which focused on achievement and accomplishment through prayer and real, deep-rooted faith.

DREAMERS FROM THE BIBLE

What kind of dream should you dream? How big should it be? Well, your dream should be bigger than you, something that dominates and consumes you. If you look through the Bible you see that those who accepted their dreams are those who were able to do the impossible. Jacob, Joseph, Daniel and John are a few examples of those with whom God shared dreams and who were willing to let those dreams drive them to success. Joel 3:28 says "I will pour out my spirit upon all flesh, and your daughters shall prophesy, your old men shall dream dreams and your young men shall see visions." Dare to dream and dare to succeed.

If you want great results and accomplishments, then it is necessary to have great faith. Life by its nature is difficult. There will be times when your faith is the only thing that will sustain you; it will be the only thing that can keep you from going over the deep end. Even though it is difficult, if you have faith and a big dream, life can become the most wonderful and fantastic adventure that you could ever experience. But it's up to you. A big dream mixed with confidence, determination, persistence and massive faith can make life the most wonderful adventure you've ever experienced, but you must use all the ingredients and you must believe that it is possible!

Don't Be Intimidated By The Obstacles

Once you set your goal and start on your way to achieve it, you will surely encounter difficulty. There will be some obstacles, but you can't allow them to intimidate you. When Moses brought the Hebrew children out of Egypt he sent 12 spies to check out the land. Ten came back saying the land flowed with milk and honey but also had giants. Those ten spies wanted to give up because they felt they were grasshoppers next to the giants. Only two put their faith in God. They were not intimidated by the giants because they had greater faith in God. They were willing to trust God and say that they could possess the land. Don't be intimidated by the obstacles. When God is for you, He's greater than the whole world against you!

$10,000 FAITH

When we look at motivation we must realize that it is very different from inspiration. Motivation deals with the head while inspiration comes from the heart. Inspiration ignores logic and ignores the circumstances. It relies on faith. If you haven't got faith you need to get faith. If you have faith then you must work to develop your faith, strengthen your faith, help it to grow stronger. Develop mountain-moving faith! Many times we try to get ten thousand dollar results on ten cent faith. If you want great results, you must have great dreams and great faith; great faith in God and a confidence that no matter what life throws at you, he will never leave you or forsake you. Then you've got to believe in yourself. You got to have the faith to believe that if you can dream it, you can do it. If you don't believe in you, don't expect others to believe in you! If you want something in life then you've got to see it, think it, dream it, believe it and go for it. And to make it a reality you've got to have faith. Remember that all things are possible if you can just believe!

One of my favorite Bible scriptures is taken from Deuteronomy, the 30th chapter, where it is written, "I call heaven and earth to witness against you that today I have set before you life and death, blessings or curses. Oh that you would choose life, that you and your children might live!" We must choose to be happy, choose to be healthy, chose to be secure and choose to be wealthy. Why do I say choose? Because success is a choice, not a chance.

After having faith in God, we must extend our faith to a solid belief in ourselves. You must believe that it is possible to achieve not only what others call improbable, but also what others see as impossible. You must have a belief in self that makes you confident, without being arrogant. Faith is the belief in what is unseen at the moment, but which is possible for the future.

Not only are there different names for faith but there are also different levels or sizes of faith. There are people who have small faith and people who have great faith. You can have mosquito faith and mosquito dreams or elephant faith and elephant dreams. A mosquito can create and gestate a baby mosquito in a few days, while an elephant takes 23 months to create a new baby elephant. What kind of faith and dreams do you want? Small overnight mosquito dreams or BIG, MASSIVE ELEPHANT-SIZED DREAMS?

Reach For It!

If you need a spiritual blessing, you should come
  expecting, as you reach, reach for it, to receive
  it by faith.
If you soul needs reviving, you'll gain strength in
  your striving, as you reach, reach for it, to
  receive it by faith.
Oh reach for it, just reach for it,
The Lord has a blessing in store for you.
All you've got to do is reach for it,
As He reaches out His hand to give it to you.

They that hunger, they that thirst after God's
  righteousness,
You should reach for it, to receive it by faith.
And for those who need deliverance don't let
  satan be a hinderance, as you reach, reach for
  it, to receive it by faith.

Reach for it, just reach for it,
The Lord has a blessing in store for you.
All you've go to do is reach for it,
As he reaches out His hand to give it to you.

We have all heard the old saying that God helps those who help themselves. This is often mistaken for scripture but in reality it was a statement made by Benjamin Franklin. Although it is not located in the Bible or from the Bible, it does have Biblical significance. If you have the faith to believe, then you can release the power of God to take action in your life. It is like the old saying, "If you take one step, God will take two." We must have faith and act on that faith to receive the full measure we are capable of receiving.

Throughout the Bible there are numerous examples of people who used their faith to release the power of God in their lives. They experienced miracles and supernatural evidences of the power of God, simply by taking action on their faith. Those miracles didn't just happen to the people in the Bible but have continued to happen throughout the years and are still happening today.

JANE REESE-COULBOURNE

I was travelling to a speaking engagement in Texas when I had the opportunity to meet a charming young lady named Jane Reese-Coulbourne. Jane just happened to be seated next to me on the plane (I told you I don't believe in luck). We struck up a conversation about the food and how surprisingly good it was. We went on to speak about the amount of travelling we both were doing, and as we spoke I realized that her schedule was far more hectic than mine. I asked how she kept up such a pace, and she said she didn't mind at all because she was simply glad to be alive.

She went on to tell me that she was so excited about life because five years earlier she had been diagnosed with breast cancer, in fact stage three breast cancer. She was in her mid-30s and just could not believe it was happening to her. She had no family history of breast cancer, she ate well and most of all she felt she was simply too young to have cancer. Her test results showed that the cancer had spread from the breast to the lymph nodes and the prognosis was not good. She was given two years to live, if that long. Jane heard the predictions but she had something else that she relied on, her faith in God. She was told that she would need at least 10 chemotherapy treatments and then would need radiation treatment. Jane continued to think positively and continued to trust God. After five treatments, Jane went back for her regular check-up and there was absolutely no sign of the cancer. The doctors could not believe it. Extensive tests were taken and extensive biopsies were performed but there were still no signs. Five years have come and gone with still no sign of cancer!

Jane is now a stage three breast cancer survivor who was faced with a hopeless situation and yet held on to her hope and faith. She never gave up hope; she looked death in the eye and won. Remember all things are possible to those who believe.

Success Is Not A Chance, It Is A Choice!

You say you cannot choose what happens to you, so how can you choose to be successful? Well, first let's define success. Napoleon Hill, the father of success and author of *Think and Grow Rich,* defines success as, "the ongoing realization of a worthwhile goal or ideal." Ongoing means you are making measurable progress towards your dream. Worthwhile means that it is good and positive and helpful to our society. Hitler was not a success because his dream was wicked and evil. He was a destroyer of society rather than a builder. Success is an ongoing realization of a worthwhile goal or ideal. As you notice, I did not say anything about money, because we have already said that success is not determined by money. There are successful mothers and fathers who have dreamed about raising honest, industrious children, and they have achieved it. Successful teachers who may not be rich but have changed the lives of young people in a positive way.

But how can success be a choice? Well, there are many things in life you cannot control, but you do have control over how you respond to them. You cannot control the weather or natural disasters, but you do control how you respond to them. You cannot control the economy but you do control how you respond to it. Success is not a chance, it is a choice. Rheinhold Neihbor said, "Lord grant me the serenity to accept the things I cannot change, the courage to change the things I can, and the wisdom to know the difference." Choose to be happy, healthy and wealthy. And remember that all things are possible if you can just believe.

Whatever You Do, It's Up To You, You Make The Difference!

No matter how you put it, no matter how you look at it, there is a specific bottom line in life. The bottom line is that whether you succeed or whether you fail, in the end it is up to you. When all is said and done (and usually, much more is said than done), success is a matter of choice, not chance.

It is true that we cannot determine what happens to us, the problems and circumstances that consistently challenge us. But we can determine how we react and respond to those situations. The results we get are a matter of the choices we make, and the choices we make are up to us and we must ultimately take responsibility for those choices. What we are and where we are result directly from the choices we make.

THE FAULT IS NOT IN THE STARS

"The fault, dear Brutus, is not in our stars; it is in ourselves, that we are underlings!" This quote reveals an age-old truth—we hold the key to our destiny. It is not what happens to you in life; it is what you do about what happens to you. It is not the stars or horoscopes that will ultimately determine your destiny; it is you and your attitude to life that ultimately determine your altitude in life. I have a sign above my desk that I read daily that says it best: "Up to a point everybody's life is shaped by environment, heredity, movement, and changes in the world around them. But then there comes a time when it lies within your grasp to shape the clay of your life into the sort of thing you wish to be. Only the weak blame their parents, their race, their times, lack of good fortune or the quirks of fate. Everyone has the power within them to say, this is what I am today and that is what I shall be tomorrow. The dream, however, must be implemented by deeds." If it is to be, then it is up to you and me to make our dreams into realities.

HUMPTY DUMPTY

Humpty Dumpty sat on a wall,
Humpty Dumpty had a great fall.
All the king's horses and all the king's men
Couldn't put Humpty together again.
(or wouldn't put Humpty together again.)

Whatever the case, the bottom line is that Humpty Dumpty ended up on the ground broken, busted and totally disgusted and it was at that point that Humpty Dumpty had to make a critical decision: to end up as a scrambled egg or sunny side up. It doesn't matter what happens to you in life; it only matters what you do about it. Sometimes in life we are going to have problems that overwhelm us, problems that are painful, difficult and will knock us down. We might be down but we do not have to be out. There may be no one able or willing to help us but ourselves. That is when we must take full responsibility for ourselves. Jesse Jackson said, "You may not be responsible for getting knocked down, but you are responsible for getting back up!" It does not matter what happens to you; it only matters what you do about it!

I learned a great lesson about responsibility when I hired an agent to handle my bookings. I turned over all responsibility for my bookings to the agent and waited for the bookings to roll in. I waited and I waited and the phone never rang. So I fired that agent and hired another. Again, I waited and I waited and again the phone never rang. It finally hit me. It is their job to get me bookings but it is my responsibility. If they do not get me bookings then they lose their job. But if they do not get me bookings I lose my house. My success is ultimately up to me, and no one else.

IT'S MY RESPONSIBILITY

Hannibal said, "If you can't find a way, make a way!" Life is not easy and there will always be obstacles in our way. No matter what we try to achieve, there will always be obstacles. The great rewards usually have great obstacles. We must have steadfast determination to make it happen. We must decide to become the director, producer, scriptwriter and star of our own lives. We must decide to dissolve into the mainstream or choose to be distinct. George Bernard Shaw said people are always blaming their circumstances for what they are. He said I don't believe in circumstances. The people who get on in this world are the people who get up and look for the circumstances they want and if they can't find them, they make them. We must take responsibility for our success or our failure; we must take responsibility for what we make out of our lives. As stated in the poem *Invictus,* by William Ernest Henley, "It matters not how straight the gate nor charged with punishment the scroll, I am the master of my fate, I am the captain of my soul." Ultimately it is up to you and to me to make our dreams into realities.

Once you accept responsibility and start the process of pursuing your dreams there will be unplanned problems and challenges that spring up and disrupt your progress. What do you do then? Well, those are the times when you must learn to "roll with the punches" and be determined to win anyway.

I was invited to speak in Kentucky for a college convocation. I was scheduled to be at the school for approximately 18 hours, arriving around 9 p.m. on Sunday evening and leaving the next day at three in the afternoon. The speech was scheduled for 10 a.m. I rose early expecting to be picked up about an hour before my speech. Fifteen minutes before my expected pick-up, I received a call from the event coordinator and was asked if I had looked out my window. I said no, I had not and when I did look I saw the ground was covered with eight inches of snow! During the night the area had been hit with a snow storm and the city was shut down, including the college. All activities had been cancelled, including my speech! All the roads out of the city were closed, and the Governor had declared a state of emergency. I was told the airport was closed and the roads to the airport would be closed for at least the next three days. I WAS STUCK!

I looked at my schedule and realized that I had a full week of speeches scheduled, and I was not going to be able to get to them. The coordinator apologized and asked if I would be okay. I told him I was fine and there was no need for him to apologize. First, I have found that there is no need to worry or get upset about things that I cannot control. It is a waste of time and energy. Second, I may not be able to choose what happens to me, but I can choose what I do about it and how I respond to it. I choose to be happy. I choose to be calm and collected. And I choose to make the best of a bad situation.

Upon realizing I was really stuck, I made some calls and rearranged my schedule. I then asked the program coordinator if someone could get me to the campus, because I had a book to finish. Those four days became a Godsend, because I finally found some time to commit to this book. I got more done in those four days than I had been able to accomplish in months!

After the weather cleared and I prepared to leave, I shared the following story with the coordinator. It has become one of my favorite ways to show that with every blessing there is a burden, and with every burden there is a blessing.

ALL THINGS WORK TOGETHER FOR GOOD . . .

Once upon a time there was a wise Chinese father in a small community. This wise father was held in high esteem, not so much because of his wisdom, but because of his two possessions—a strong son and a horse. He was particularly esteemed for the horse because he was the only person in the community with one. One day the horse broke through the fence and ran away. All the neighbors came around and said, "What bad luck!" And the father replied, "Why do you call it bad luck?" A few days later the horse returned with 10 other horses! And all the neighbors said, "What good luck!" And the wise father responded, "Why do you call it good luck?" Soon after his strong son went to the corral to break one of the new horses, and was thrown and broke his hip. All the neighbors came and said, "What bad luck!" And the wise father responded, "Why do you call it bad luck?" Later the evil warlord came through the town and gathered all of the strong, able-bodied young men and took them off to war. The only one he did not take was the boy with the broken hip. All the young men were killed in battle.

When the news reached the community, the neighbors rushed to the father and said, "What good luck!" And the father said "Why do you call it good luck? Don't you know all things work together for good for those who love the Lord!"

There may be times when things really look tough and when things do not go as you planned, but if you look hard enough and have faith, you will see that with every blessing there is a burden and with every burden, there is a blessing. Every dark cloud has a silver lining, if you are willing to look for it and learn from it.

The next question I usually get is, "Okay, I understand all of that, but I was dealt a bad hand. I have no control over the hand I was dealt, so what do I do now?" Well it is true you cannot control the hand you were dealt, but you can control what you do with that hand and how you respond to whatever you are faced with. Ultimately it is always up to you whether you win or lose. You sometimes might lose the battle, but do not confuse the battle with the war. To the victor go the spoils, and the victor is usually the one who refuses to give up; the one who makes the conscious decision to face the obstacles, look them square in the eye, fight on and never give up.

Statistics show that worry is a major contributor to illnesses. Worry and anxiety not only contribute to heart disease and high blood pressure but also to arthritis, rheumatism, hypertension and a lot of other illnesses. Statistics also indicate that married people live longer than single people, probably because they have someone with whom to share their concerns and anxieties. Worry not only shortens your life, but it is of no use in your search for excellence. You gain nothing substantive by worrying except sickness, pain and self doubt. Scripture says worry does not add one iota to your life, not one hair to your head! Don't worry, be happy . . . because you make the choice!

DON'T WORRY, BE HAPPY!

Don't worry, be happy! Choose to be happy for you ultimately make the choice. You can either choose to worry about life and what will happen in the future or you can choose to be happy, to enjoy life and to live life to the fullest. It is a choice. The word worry comes from the word "to choke," to strangle. It is an extension of fear. Fear is crippling. It shackles those who could do great things and keeps them from even attempting. Fear chokes and kills dreams and creativity. And the most interesting thing about fear is that it is a learned behavior! Psychologists state that there are only two fears that we are born with: the fear of falling and the fear of loud sounds. All other fears are learned! They are usually a misuse of the imagination. The imagination was created for us to dream and see positive things that are not yet reality, and see them as a possibility.

Many times in life we use our minds to think of every possible problem that could arise. Our minds are created not to think up problems but rather to think up solutions. After thinking up the solutions our minds are then to be used to think about how to make those dreams into realities. Don't let fear choke you. Release your fear, bust it, break it, forsake it, leave it and let it go. Look fear in the eye. Challenge it and it will go away! Fear cannot stand action. Go after your dreams. Don't worry; dream it and do it. Choose to be happy.

If you want to be a success, then you must throw away worry and doubt and get on with your life. Each day live life with gusto and strive to be the best you can possibly be. Choose to be happy and always seek excellence in all that you do. Not perfection, but excellence. Why? Because perfection will frustrate and debilitate you, while excellence is an ongoing focus on being the best you can be. In pursuing excellence you can continue to better your best and break your personal records, without the frustration of not being perfect. We should always want to better what we did yesterday, improve what we accomplished in the past and get stronger from each level of accomplishment.

EXCELLENCE COSTS

I read a sign that said, "Excellence costs. You must pay the price in full, but you reap outstanding returns on your investment." There is a price for excellence. It is not cheap, but the returns are outstanding because they continue to bring dividends. Excellence is like truth; no matter how much you push it down and try to cover it up, it will always rise to the top. It cannot be denied. It is like the Phoenix that rises from the ashes. No matter how you try to destroy and disrupt it, excellence will always rise! Life is difficult for everyone, the rain falls on the righteous as well as the unrighteous. But those who believe in excellence and pursue it with passion are those who are not overcome by the vicissitudes of life. Don't just *go* through problems and challenges but rather *grow* through them. Excellence costs . . . but pays outstanding rewards.

You must dream, make a conscious determined decision, take action and finally strive for excellence in your pursuit. Yet, we see people who could be great and who could do amazing things, but don't, due to a lack of desire. Desire is the element that separates the men from the boys, the girls from the women and the achievers from the mere dreamers. Desire is the element that some call "the little extra that makes the big difference." You've got to want to be a success. You've got to want to be excellent. You must want to make your dreams into realities and achieve greatness. You've got to want it and want it bad!

I was speaking at a school last fall where I met a six foot five, 250 pound young man. He was a great physical specimen. After the program I asked him what he wanted to be and he told me that he wanted to play football. I told him he definitely had the physique but did he have the desire, the drive, the determination since professional football is so competitive. He said he wanted it badly. I said, "How bad?" and he said, "Real bad." Then I asked the definitive question, "Do you want it badly enough to go through a brick wall?" He replied, "No, I don't want it that badly." I told him until he developed the desire to want it that badly it would be difficult for him to achieve it because mere talent and ability is still not enough. There are people all across this country who are not using their talents to the fullest. They are working jobs they settled for because the competition was too tough and they didn't have that little bit of extra "umph" to rise above the masses. They didn't have that little bit extra that made the big difference; they didn't have the desire. They didn't want it badly enough!

Les Brown, "The Motivator" says, "You gotta be hungry." I say, "You've got to want it so badly that you are willing to go through a brick wall." You may never have to go through that brick wall but you must be willing if it's necessary. To be a success at any level, you must want it bad! The great football coach, Vince Lombardi said, "The difference between a successful person and others is not a lack of strength, not a lack of knowledge, but rather a lack of will." DESIRE!

How Badly Do You Want It?

"So you want to be a rock star, huh?" That was a question a record company executive asked me when I walked into his office over ten years ago. He asked me if I was willing to do what it takes to become a rock star. Was I willing to leave the comforts of home? Was I willing to move to another city? Was I willing to live on the streets, if necessary, until I made it? Was I willing to get up early and stay up late? Was I willing to do whatever it takes? He said you might not have to pay that price, but you have to be willing. Well, most people are not willing to give their all to become a rock star, a doctor star, a nurse star, a computer star, a sales star, an architect star, entrepreneur star or any other kind of star. Because you have to be willing to give your all if you want your dreams to come true. This poem, written by Berton Braley, says it best:

> If you want a thing bad enough to go out and
>   fight for it
> To work day and night for it
> To give up your time, your peace and your sleep
>   for it, if all that you dream and scheme, are
>   about it.
> And life seems useless and worthless without it, If
>   you'd gladly sweat for it, and fret it, and lose all
>   of your terror of the opposition for it.
> If you simply go after that thing that you want
> With all of your capacity, strength and sagacity
> Faith, hope and confidence and stern pertinacity,
> If neither cold, poverty, famine, nor gout,

Sickness nor pain, of body and brain
Can keep you away from the thing that you want,
If dogged and grim you beseech and beset it
With the help of God you will surely get it!

Do you want it bad? Are you serious? I mean real serious? As the saying goes, "Are you as serious as a heart attack?" Because a heart attack will take you out, you cannot afford to play and half step when you deal with a heart attack because it could be your last step! Are you really serious about your success? Are you willing to go the extra mile, to do the little extra that makes the big difference? Are you willing to stay up late and get up early? Are you willing to turn off the T.V. and read? Are you willing to experience some pain and rejection as you pursue your dream? Are you willing to do what is uncomfortable, to fight for your dream? Are you serious? Are you serious about what you're doing or are you just dabbling?

Many people really think they are serious, but in reality they are just going through the motions. They have a mental image of themselves being busy and serious but in reality they are just fooling themselves. They are active but going nowhere—like running on a treadmill, running fast yet still in the same spot! People kid themselves not realizing the difference between activity and results. How do I know? I was one of those people, busy but going nowhere. For years I was a whirlwind of activity, but when I looked closely I hadn't accomplished anything. I was going through the motions but I wasn't really serious. I didn't want it badly enough.

When you are serious you are willing to go the extra mile and give the extra little bit. You are willing to get up earlier and fight for your dreams, every day. You are willing to do what is physically uncomfortable. Your commitment rises to another level. You look for ways to consistently improve your best effort. You dig in and make a decision to become steadfast, unmovable and unstoppable, no matter what it takes!

Ask yourself the question, "What would I do, if I were serious?" What goals would I pursue? What things would I continue to do and what would I discontinue? What nonproductive, time-wasting activities would I eliminate? What would I do if I were really serious? Ask yourself the question and your mind will give you the answer. Once you get the answers, take out a sheet of paper and write them down. Read them and start to work on the list. Realize that no matter what you are presently doing, you can do more. You can accomplish and achieve more, if you willing to get serious.

Friends, pursue excellence in all that you do. Develop great desire and commitment to reach your goals and then take full responsibility for your success. Get serious, and in short order you will start to see you dreams begin to sprout, grow and blossom!

ONE MOMENT IN TIME!

One Moment In Time
by Albert Hammond and John Bettis

Each day I live, I want to be
A day to give the best of me
I'm only one, but not alone
My finest day is yet unknown

I broke my heart for every gain
To taste the sweet, I faced the pain
I rise and fall, yet through it all
This much remains

I want one moment in time
When I'm more than I thought I could be
When all of my dreams are a heartbeat away
And the answers are all up to me

Give me one moment in time
When I'm racing with my destiny
Then in that one moment of time,
I will feel, I will feel eternity.

In everybody's life, there are those moments that define the direction and context of their lives. Those moments are commonly called defining moments, those brief, tiny minutes that alter our lives and thereby alter the lives of others. Rosa Parks had a defining moment one day in 1955 in Montgomery, Alabama, when she refused to give up her seat on a bus, because she was tired. She made a decision that moment which sparked a movement that ultimately changed this country. Another defining moment was during the desperate search for someone to lead the Montgomery people in a bus boycott. A young 26-year-old preacher said, "I'll do it," and the world would never be the same because Martin Luther King, Jr., made a decision to step forward and change his destiny.

It was a defining moment when the Apostle Paul had an encounter on the Damascus road which changed his life and the world. In a moment he went from being a persecutor of the Christians to the greatest defender of the faith. It happened in just a moment. It was also a defining moment when the thief we spoke of earlier was hanging on a cross next to Jesus and realized that he could change his life if he would just say, "Remember me, when you come into your kingdom."

We all have defining moments in our lives, moments that change the emphasis of our existence and alter the direction of our lives. Some would say our destiny is determined in those moments. Yet many of us shy away from them and back off from the decisions that must be made in those moments, because they are uncomfortable. Defining moments are by their nature uncomfortable, but growth is uncomfortable, change is uncomfortable, life is uncomfortable. Yet those defining moments are the moments that create winners.

Franklin Delano Roosevelt had a defining moment the day he woke up and realized his legs wouldn't move for he had been stricken by polio. Yet he made the decision to keep going after his dream. He went on to become one of the most popular presidents this nation has ever known and the only president ever elected four times.

Winston Churchill had a defining moment as a child when his classmates teased him because of his severe stuttering problem. He made up his mind to prove to the world he had something to say and would say it! He overcame his stuttering and became a gifted orator, a national leader and eventually the prime minister of England. He won the Nobel Peace Prize and became one of the most quoted speakers of our time!

DENNIS BYRD

In 1992 Dennis Byrd was a very popular defensive lineman for the New York Jets. One Sunday he was in a freak accident involving one of his teammates. From that moment on his life was forever changed. He remained on the ground after the collision unable to move his hands or feet. The doctors and team trainers ran onto the field. After a brief explanation they realized he had no feeling from his neck down. Initially they thought it was a "Stinger," a condition that temporarily deadens the nerves. After a few days it was apparent this was not a temporary condition. The doctors gave him a battery of tests and concluded he would never walk again. But Dennis Byrd was not a typical patient and didn't accept those conditions. Dennis Byrd had overcome obstacles just to get the opportunity to play professional football, for he had been told he would never be good enough. He had something that was greater than any obstacle he would face, his great faith in God and in himself.

In all the interviews while he was still in the hospital, he continued to say that his faith would bring him through. He never gave up that belief. Today he is president of the Dennis Byrd Foundation. In the fall of 1993 Dennis Byrd was honored by the New York Jets for his courage and commitment to excellence. On that day Dennis Byrd returned to the same field where he had experienced his defining moment and had been paralyzed. On that day Dennis Byrd walked onto the field under his own strength without a cane or a walker, due only to his great faith and great determination. Faith is the key. Believe and receive.

Faith is the essence of things hoped for and the evidence of things not seen. When we have those moments that define us we must realize that faith is the ingredient which galvanizes those times into life changing moments. Dr. Robert Schuller shared one of his defining moments and how it changed his life. He told how he had gone to California in 1953 to start a church and was led to use the only place he could find, a drive-in theater. He planned to use that location only until he could save enough money to get a chapel. He started the church and because of its unique nature he got some unique members, like Rosie Gray, who couldn't attend regular churches because they were not equipped for handicapped members. Rosie attended Rev. Shuller's church and was an important part of it.

Finally Rev. Schuller was ready to move to his chapel, but what would he do with Rosie? He was faced with a tough decision, open the new chapel or stay at the drive-in and limit his growth. It was at that point that he had a defining moment. He realized that his mission was to serve and he couldn't limit nor exclude people in his service. He choose to expand to the new chapel but also to continue the drive-in service, and to make plans to build a new facility that was a combination church and drive-in worship center. He went on to purchase the land for a new church and in that quest he had to cash in his life insurance, mortgage his home, sell his car and borrow to the limit. The result is the Crystal Cathedral and Dr. Schuller's Hour of Power, which is a world-wide ministry that has changed the lives of countless millions. His defining moment changed his life and changed the lives of others. It was a moment defined because of a small handicapped woman named Rosie Gray.

Nathan Hale had a defining moment that charged a movement. During the Revolutionary War Nathan Hale volunteered for a very dangerous mission behind enemy lines. While on his return from the mission he was captured and sentenced to death within 24 hours. He was not allowed any communication with others and his hand-written note to his parents was torn up in front of his eyes. Yet at the moment he ascended the stairs to be hanged he made a statement that changed the whole mood of the war effort. "I only regret that I have only one life to lose for my country." He was only 21 years old but had the courage and calmness of mind well beyond his years. At that moment he sparked a rally that inspired the revolutionary forces and pushed them on to win despite the odds. And those words have continued to inspire countless generations of Americans since!

We all have defining moments that have altered our direction. But they only become defining moments when they actually define and shape our character and perspective. It is really not the moment that defines but our response to the moment that makes the difference. We all have unexpected moments that alter our histories, but many run from them and wilt in the heat. They refuse to rise to the challenges of the moment. W Mitchell experienced one of those moments when he was involved in the fire that changed his life, but he rose to the occasion and made the decision to win in spite of the odds, and went on to greatness. Walt Disney had one of those moments when his business was taken from him and he lost all of his trusted staff and had to start completely over from scratch. He rose to the occasion and went on to greatness.

I've had moments that have defined and developed my personality and my character. Like the day I grew up and changed from a boy to a man. It was a sunny October day in 1970. I rushed home from school to change clothes for an evening ball game and ran into the house to find my father on the floor unconscious. He was not breathing and unresponsive to my calls. I called 911 and calmly told the operator my father was lying on the floor unconscious. Then I called my mother at work and told her she should come home because all was not well (so as not to frighten her even though I was well aware of the situation). When my mother arrived, the paramedics had taken his body and I was left to comfort my mother and tell my brother that dad had died. I grew up that day.

The other defining moment was when I went from being a good, but limited, local performer, to taking the first step to being a performer who had the potential for greatness. I was invited to perform at a showcase in Nashville, Tennessee. I went with the attitude that I was God's gift to the music industry. I would dazzle them with my showmanship and not worry about the actual singing. Well, it was a disaster! I was a flop, a dud! The walk from the stage that night was the loneliest walk I had ever taken in my life. I was used to the crowd cheering and now I was getting nothing but silence. I realized at that moment the problem was not my talent but rather how I had chosen to use my talents. I had tried to simply impress and share nothing of substance, when I should have entertained to encourage, inspire and change lives for the better. I was merely going through the motions. A performance that has no passion and no purpose is really just an exercise in futility. I decided in that moment I would not take my talents or my audiences for granted ever again. That was a defining moment that established the seed for greater possibilities in my future. Napoleon Hill said that in every adversity are the seeds for an equal or greater opportunity. I know that statement is true!

Our defining moments are those that can define us or deflate us, make us or break us, help us or hurt us. It all depends on how we respond to the moment that makes the difference and that shapes our destiny. If we grasp the moment and *GROW* through it—not just *GO* through it, but *GROW* through it—we become stronger! If we wilt under the pressure and give up on the moment, we tend to become weaker. The old proverb says, that the same hammer that molds the steel, shatters the glass. Defining moments are unpredictable, yet they have a profound effect on our futures.

HOLD YOUR GROUND

When I was a child I remember playing a game called Uncle, where someone would play hide and seek; and when you were found they would all hold you down and tickle you until you said "Uncle" and gave up. Some of our playmates would easily give up and say Uncle, but there was another group who refused to say Uncle. No matter what you did to them, they would not say Uncle. In time, I realized that those were the same people who tended to be the leaders and the most respected by the other kids.

I learned that when you hold your ground and refuse to give in to pressure, it is going to be difficult and uncomfortable. But those who stand their ground are the ones who tend to gain the highest respect. Nelson Mandela refused to compromise, give in or give up. During his 20th year in jail, the South African government offered him his freedom, if he agreed to compromise and accept Apartheid. He had to make a decision he knew would have a profound impact on his life and the lives of the people of his country. He was getting old and his time was running out. Prison life was extremely hard and cruel. Yet he chose to stay in prison and not give in to the pressure. He held his ground and his stature grew not only among the people in South Africa but among those in other countries.

As you move among your daily pursuits there will be days when you will find yourself being asked to give up, give in and say "Uncle." The pressure will be strong and the road will be difficult, but remember someone is always looking at you, and looking to you to provide leadership. Don't give in. Don't wilt under the pressure. Hold your ground and you will grow from the experience, not only in the way others see you, but more importantly, in the way you see yourself. Remember, all things are possible if you can just believe!

I learned to hold my ground as a young boy. As I grew and matured I realized life was very unpredictable and changed rapidly. Yet the more things change, they more they stay the same. I became aware of that when I was about 14 years old and in the youth choir of Asbury United Methodist Church. We performed a piece of music called *Desiderata,* which totally intrigued me. I was amazed at how hip and cool the writer was and how much he had a pulse on the world of today. Then I found out it wasn't written in this century or the last century! I was amazed when I found out this piece was written over 500 years ago! I realized it was true, that the more things change the more they stay the same!

DESIDERATA

Go placidly amid the noise and haste. And remember what peace there may be in silence. And as far as possible without surrender, be on good terms with all persons. Speak your truth quietly and clearly and listen to others, even the dull and ignorant, they too have their stories. Avoid loud and aggressive people, they are vexations to the spirit. If you compare yourself with others you may become vain and bitter. For always there will be greater and lesser persons than yourself. Enjoy your achievements, as well as your plans. Keep interested in your own career, however humble. It is a real possession in the changing fortunes of time. Exercise caution in your business affairs, for the world is full of trickery. Let this not blind you to what virtue there is. Many persons strive for high ideals and everywhere life is full of heroism. Be yourself, especially do not feign affection, neither be cynical about love. In the face of all aridity and disenchantment, it is perennial as the grass. Take kindly the counsel of the years, gracefully surrendering the things of youth. Nurture strength of spirit to shield you in sudden misfortunes. But do not distress yourself with imaginings. Many fears are born of fatigue and loneliness. Beyond a wholesome discipline, be gentle with yourself. You are a child of the universe, no less than the trees and the stars, you have a right to be here, and whether or not it is clear to you, no doubt the universe is unfolding as it should. Therefore, be at peace with God, whatever you conceive God to be. And whatever your labors and aspirations, and the noisy confusion of life, keep peace with your soul. With all its sham, drudgery and broken dreams, strive to be happy!

BRIGHT MOMENTS

I met a travelling musician who had an impact on me even though I only had a few opportunities to talk to him. I didn't get to know him well, in fact I don't even know his real name, except that everyone called him "Bright Moments." They called him "Bright Moments" because he would always greet you by saying "Bright Moments," rather than hello. He would leave with the same statement, rather than saying goodbye. He was a very peaceful yet powerful presence, who looked in your eyes and shook your hand with genuine and sincere interest. Just from those brief moments with him I was able to learn, firsthand, about treating others as I really wanted to be treated. As quickly as he came, he left and I never saw him again but I will always remember the lessons I learned. Love life, treat others as you would like to be treated, and always be thankful, enthusiastic and excited about life. And finally, always share positive greetings and salutations with others, because as you water the plants of others you cannot help but get some water on yourself. And you to will have many "Bright Moments!" Have a Great Day!

Ladies and gentlemen, as I end this book I want to remind you of your greatness and the unlimited power you have within you. Always dream the big dreams, think the big thoughts and treat others as you would like to be treated. We are all independent, yet interdependent and interrelated. As you go forth, remember it only takes a minute to change your life. The minute you make the decision to change and overcome your fear is the moment you win the war. I send you forth to follow your dreams and go after them with all that you have within you. And I bid that you will always have "Bright Moments" every day of your life!

IF (BY RUDYARD KIPLING)

If you can keep your head when all about you
Are losing theirs and blaming it on you,
If you can trust yourself when all men doubt you,
But make allowances for their doubting too;
If you can wait and not be tired by waiting,
Or being lied about, don't deal in lies,
Or being hated, don't give away to hating,
And yet don't look too good, nor talk too wise.

If you can dream and not make dreams your
    master;
If you can think and not make thoughts your aim;
If you can meet triumph and disaster
And treat those two imposters just the same;
If you can bear to hear the truth you've spoken
Twisted by knaves to make a trap for fools,
Or watch the things you gave your life to, broken,
And stoop and build'em up with worn out tools;

If you can make one heap of all your winnings
And risk it on one turn of pitch-and-toss,
And lose, and start again at your beginnings
And never breathe a word about your loss;
If you can force your heart and nerve and sinew
To serve you turn long after they are gone,
And so hold on when there is nothing in you
Except "The will" which says to them, "Hold on!"

If you can talk to crowds and keep your virtue,
Or walk with kings, nor lose the common touch,
If neither foes not loving friends can hurt you,
If all men count with you, but none too much;
If you can fill the unforgiving minute
With sixty seconds worth of distance run,
Yours is the earth and everything that's in
   it,
And, which is more, you'll be a man, my
   son!

Remember that all things are possible if you can just believe! This is Willie Jolley. Have a great day!